# The Beatles Classic Hits

ISBN 978-0-634-02573-0

HAL•LEONARD®
CORPORATION

7777 W. BLUEMOUND RD. P.O. BOX 13819 MILWAUKEE, WI 53213

Visit Hal Leonard Online at
www.halleonard.com

# BECAUSE

Words and Music by JOHN LENNON
and PAUL McCARTNEY

Moderately slow

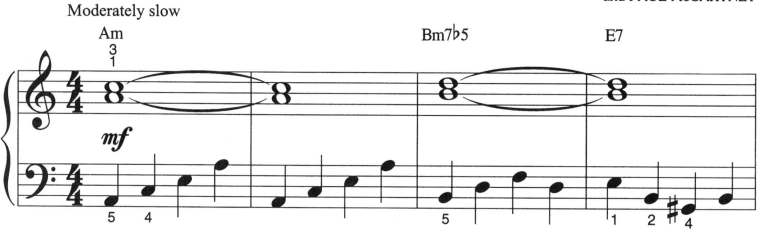

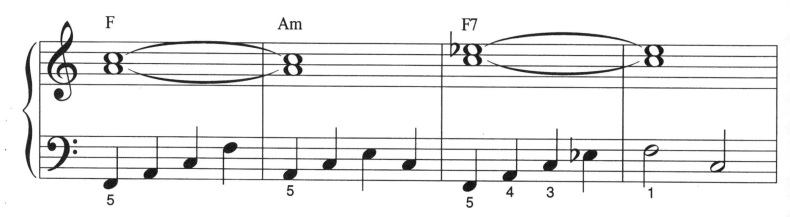

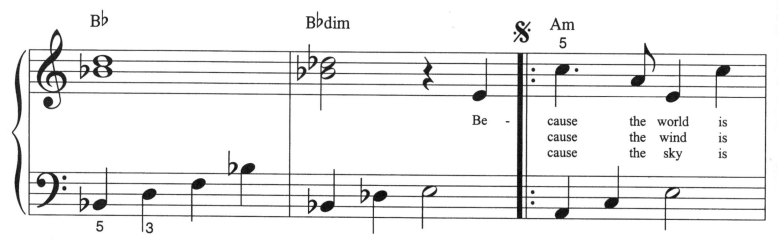

Be - cause the world is
cause the wind is
cause the sky is

round, it turns me on; be -
high, it blows my mind; be -
blue, it makes me cry; be -

F        Am        F7

cause    the    world    is    round.
cause    the    wind    is    high.
cause    the    sky    is    blue.

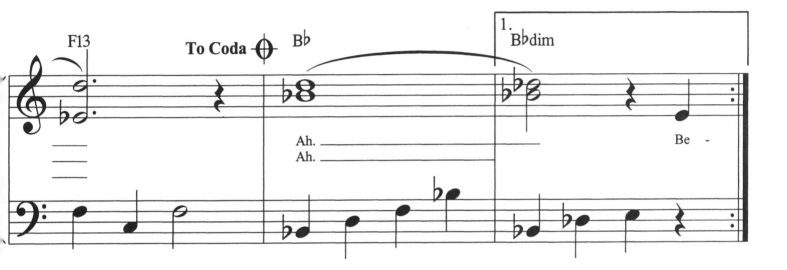

F13      **To Coda**   Bb      1. Bbdim

Ah.
Ah.
Be -

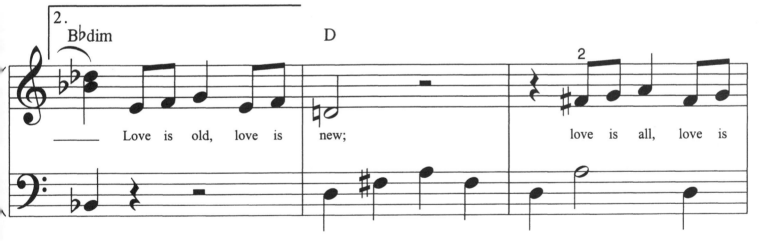

2. Bbdim      D

Love is old, love is new;      love is all, love is

E7      **D.S. al Coda**

you.      Be -

**CODA**

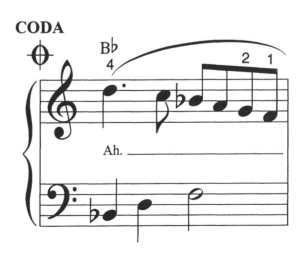

Bb

Ah.

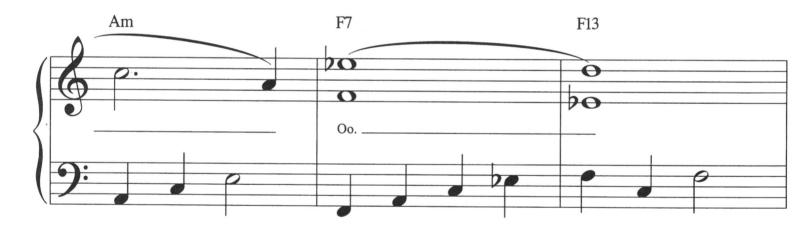

# DO YOU WANT TO KNOW A SECRET?

Words and Music by JOHN LENNON
and PAUL McCARTNEY

Slowly and freely

You'll nev - er know how much I real - ly love you.

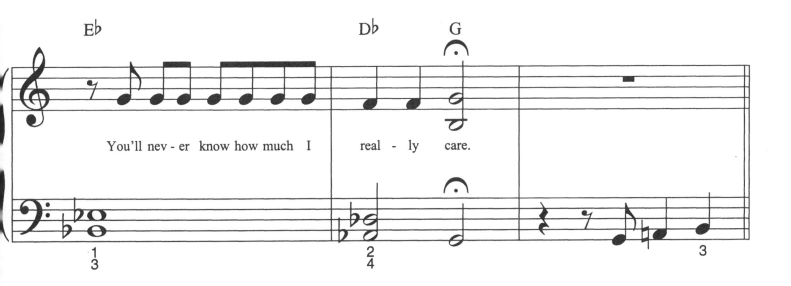

You'll nev - er know how much I real - ly care.

Moderately

Lis - ten, ___ do you want to know a se - cret?

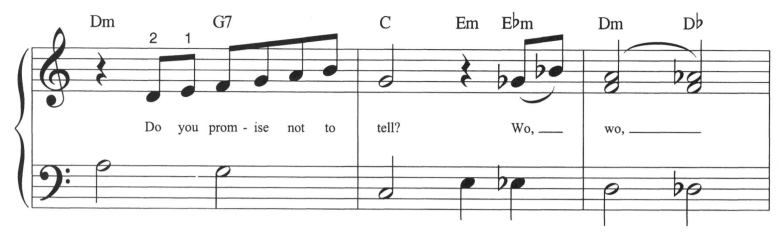

Do you prom - ise not to tell? Wo, ___ wo, ___

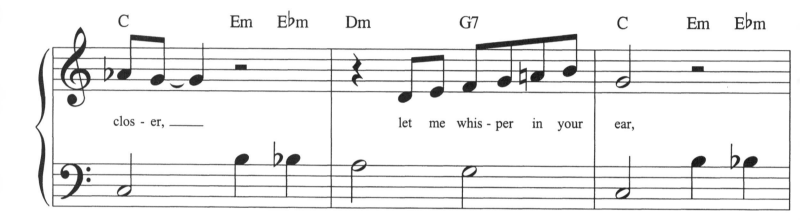

clos - er, ___ let me whis - per in your ear,

say the words you love to hear: ___ I'm in love with

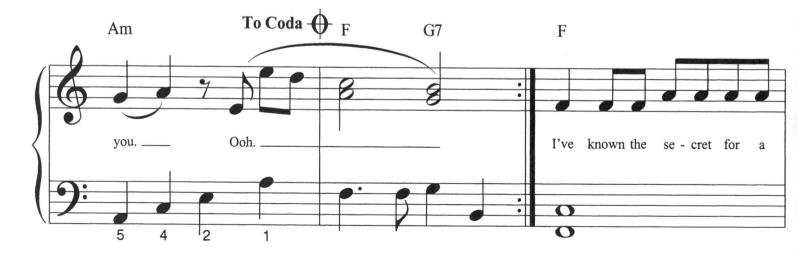

you. ___ Ooh. ___ I've known the se - cret for a

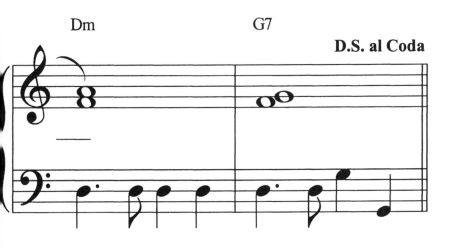

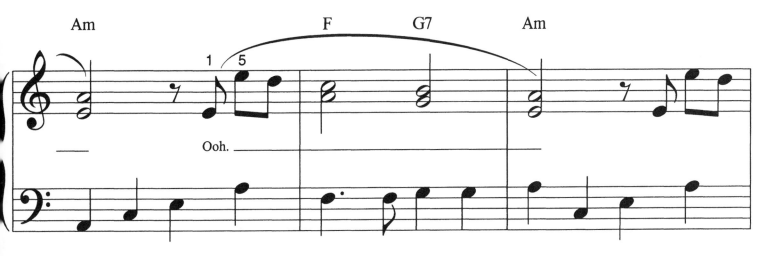

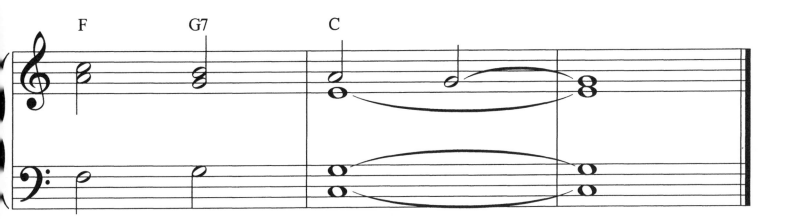

# BLACKBIRD

Words and Music by JOHN LENNON
and PAUL McCARTNEY

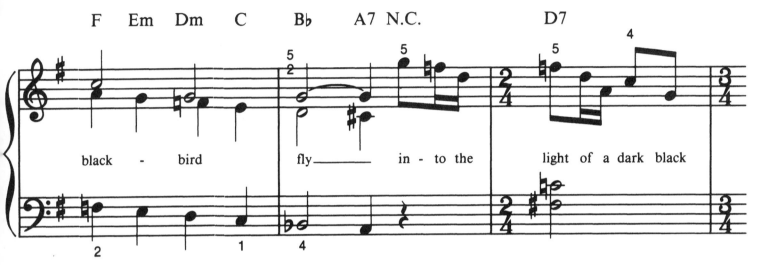

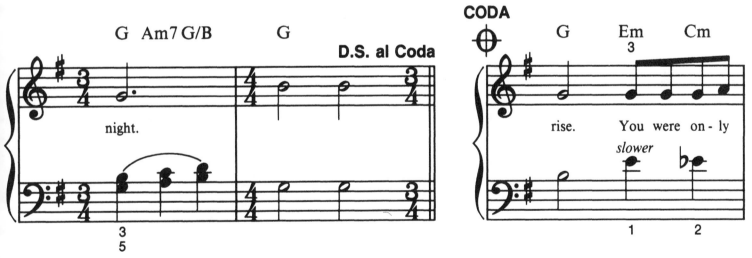

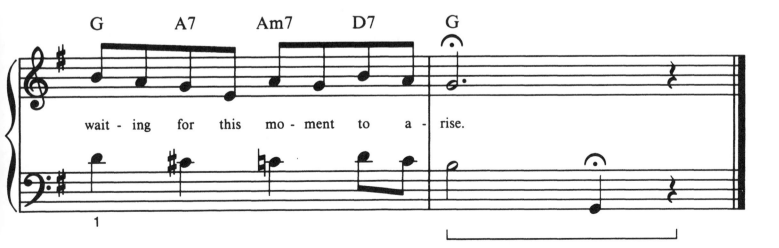

# COME TOGETHER

Words and Music by JOHN LENNON
and PAUL McCARTNEY

Moderately slow

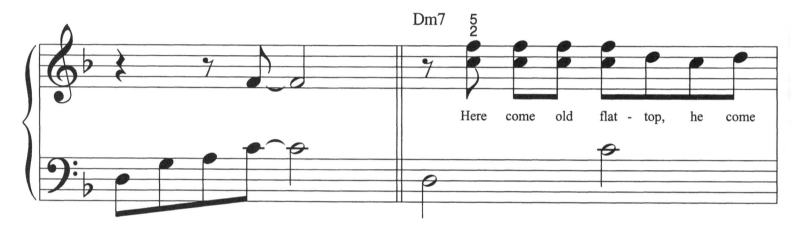

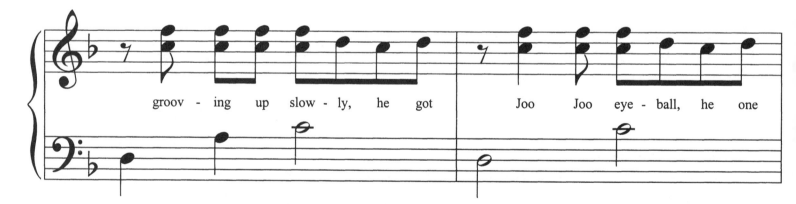

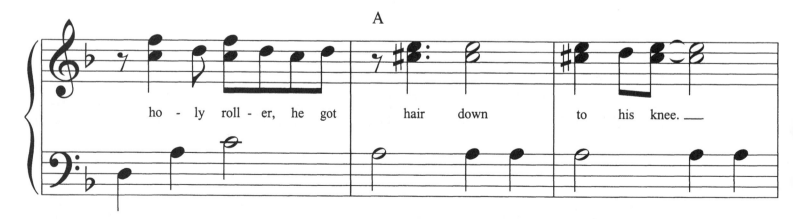

Got to be a jok - er, he just doo what he please. ___

He wear no shoe - shine, he got
He bag pro - duc - tion, he got
He roll - er coast - er, he got

toe - jam foot - ball, he got       mon - key fin - ger, he shoot
wal - rus gum - boot, he got       O - no side - board, he one
ear - ly warn - ing, he got        mud - dy wa - ter, he one

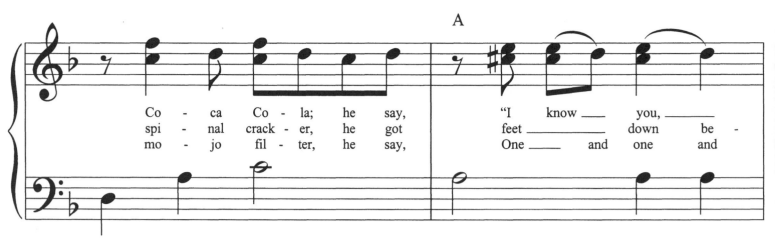

Co - ca Co - la; he say,
spi - nal crack - er, he got
mo - jo fil - ter, he say,

"I know ____ you, ____
feet ____ down be -
One ____ and one and

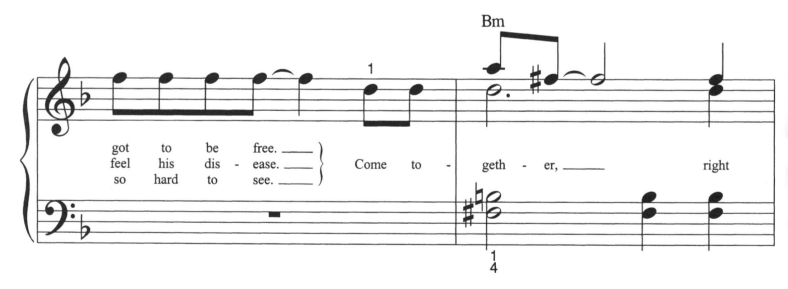

you know me." ____
low his knee. ____
one is three." ____

One thing I can tell you is you
Hold you in his arm - chair, you can
Got to be good look - ing 'cause he

got to be free. ____
feel his dis - ease. ____
so hard to see. ____

Come to - geth - er, ____ right

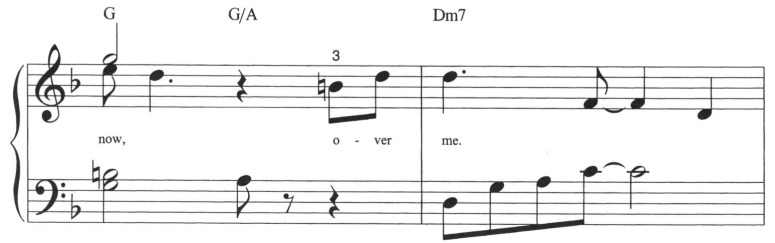

now,

o - ver me.

**Repeat 2 times**

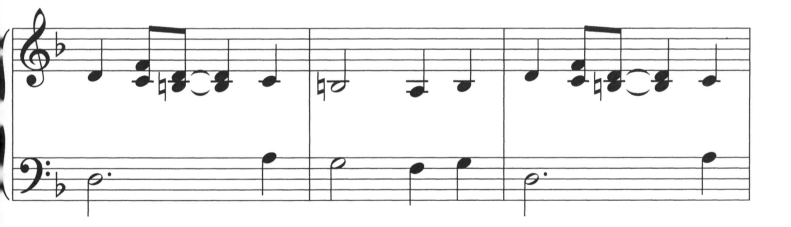

# THE FOOL ON THE HILL

Words and Music by JOHN LENNON
and PAUL McCARTNEY

Sadly

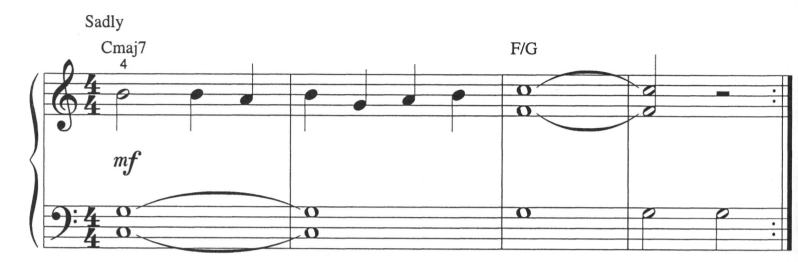

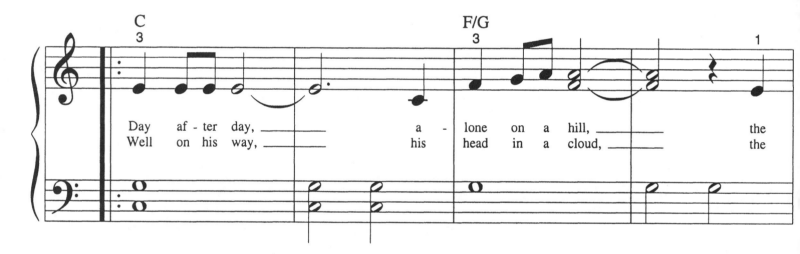

Day af-ter day, _____ a - lone on a hill, _____ the
Well on his way, _____ his head in a cloud, _____ the

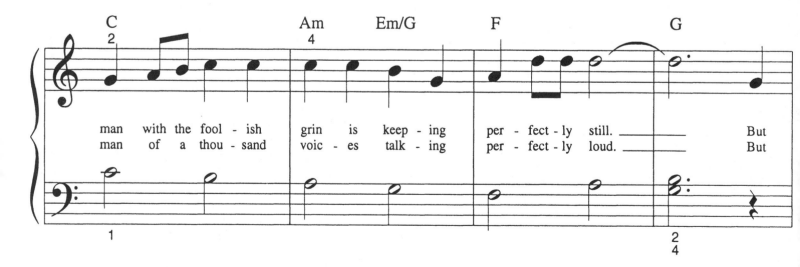

man with the fool-ish grin is keep-ing per-fect-ly still. _____ But
man of a thou-sand voic-es talk-ing per-fect-ly loud. _____ But

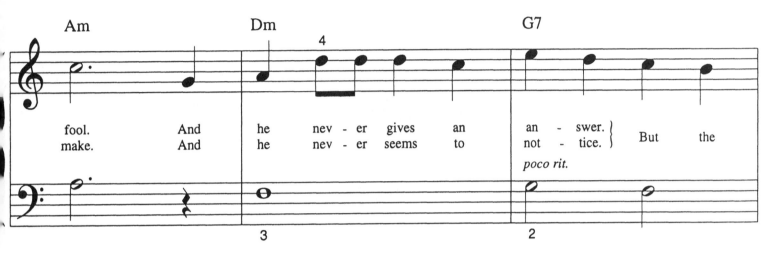

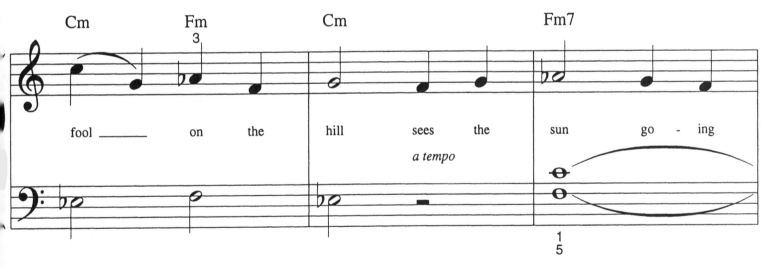

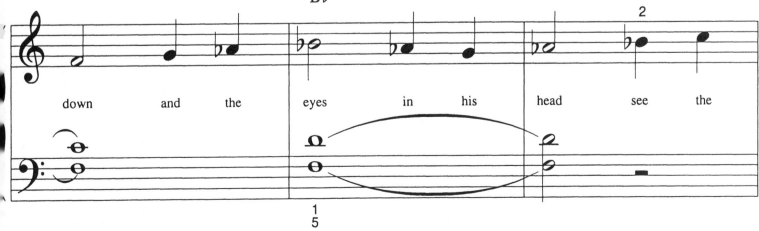

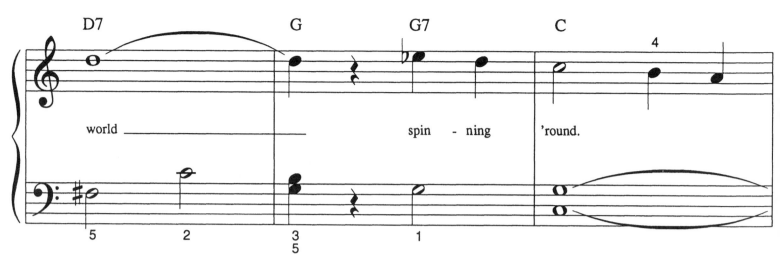

world _____ spin - ning 'round.

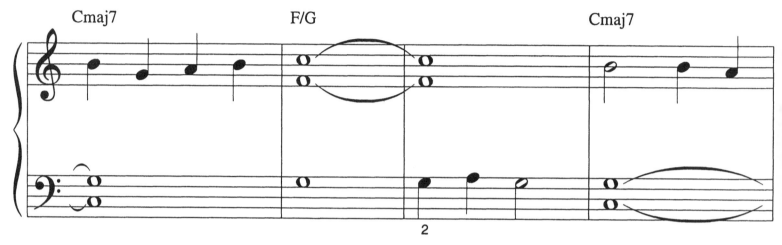

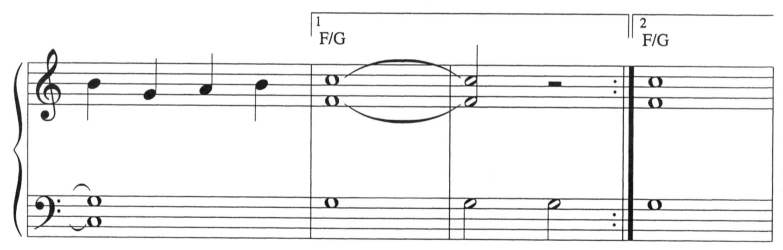

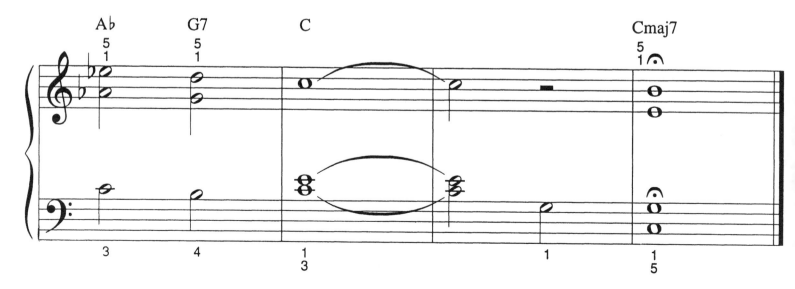

# HERE COMES THE SUN

Words and Music by
GEORGE HARRISON

Moderately

Here comes the sun, doo da doo doo,

here comes the sun, and I say "It's all right."

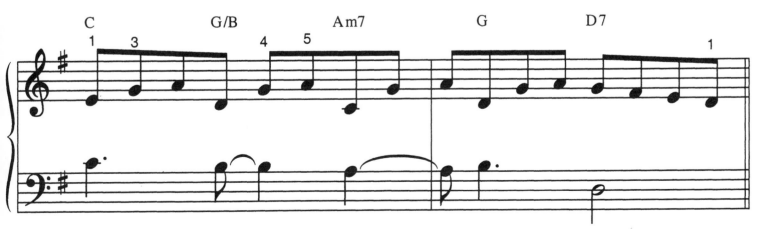

Lit - tle dar - ling,      it's been a      long, cold, lone - ly
Lit - tle dar - ling,      the smiles re - turn - ing to____ their
Lit - tle dar - ling,      I feel that      ice is slow - ly

win - ter;      lit - tle dar - ling,      it feels like
fac - es;      lit - tle dar - ling,      it seems like
melt - ing;      lit - tle dar - ling,      it seems like

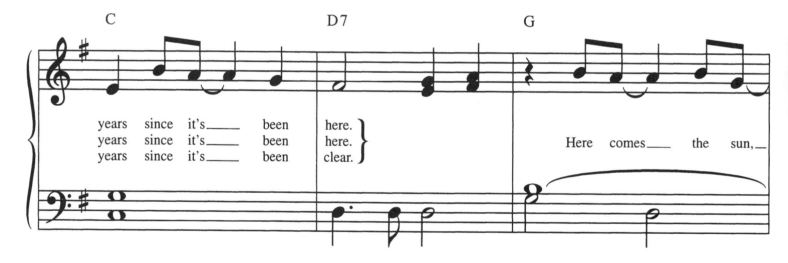

years since it's____ been here. }
years since it's____ been here. }
years since it's____ been clear. }

Here comes____ the sun,__

here comes____ the sun,____ and I say

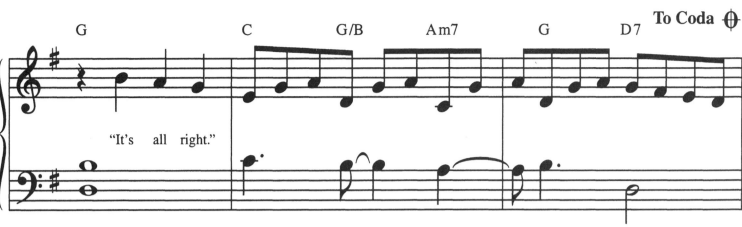

**To Coda** ⊕

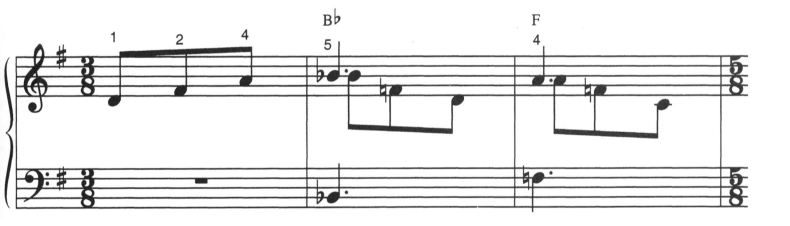

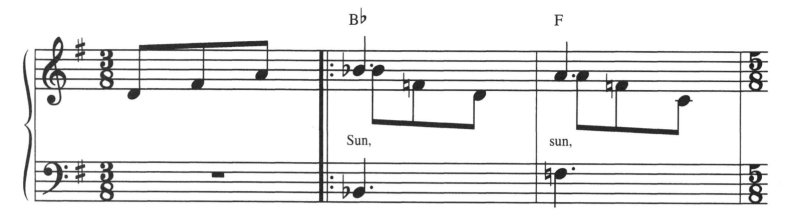

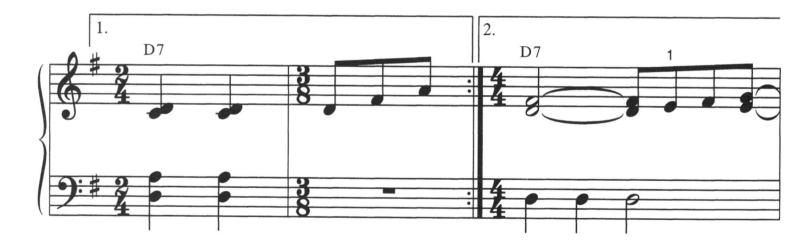

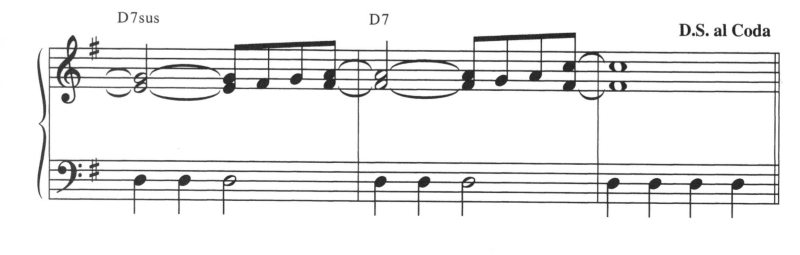

**CODA**

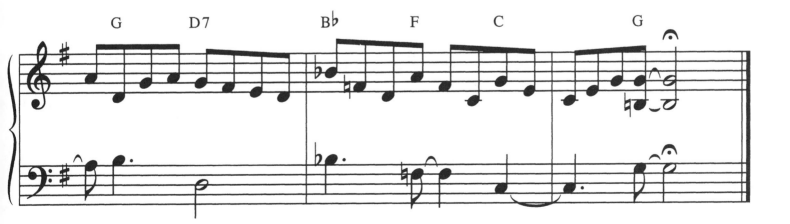

# GIRL

Words and Music by JOHN LENNON
and PAUL McCARTNEY

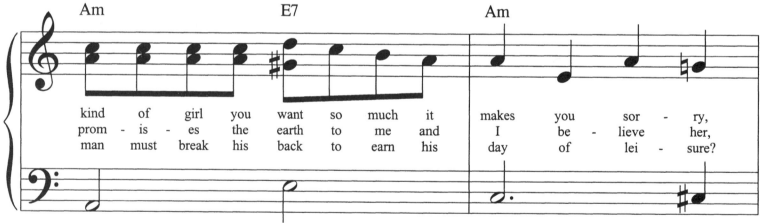

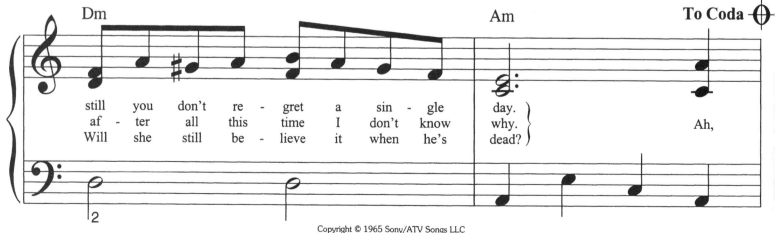

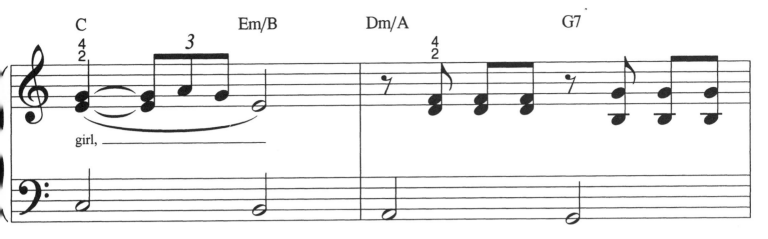

When you say she's look - ing good, she

acts as if it's un - der - stood, she's cool, _____ ooh, _____

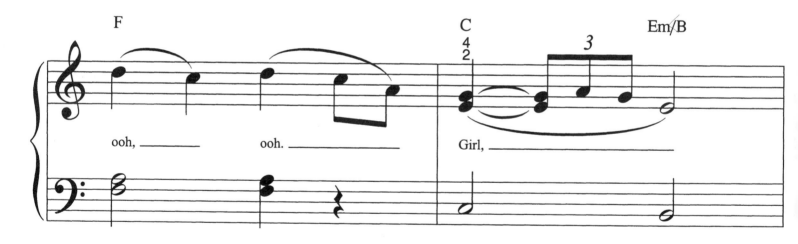

ooh, _____ ooh. _____ Girl, _____

girl, _____ girl. _____

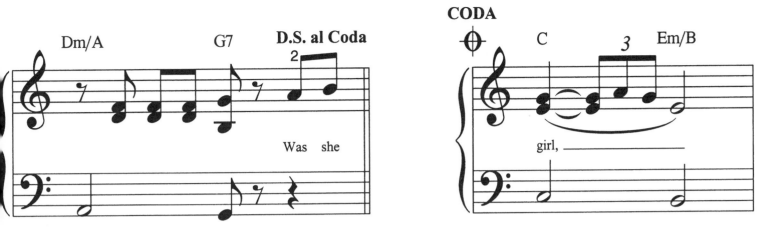

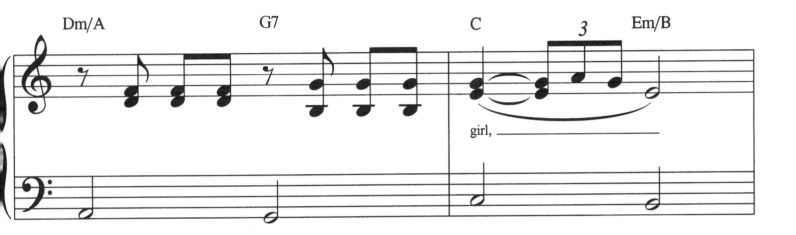

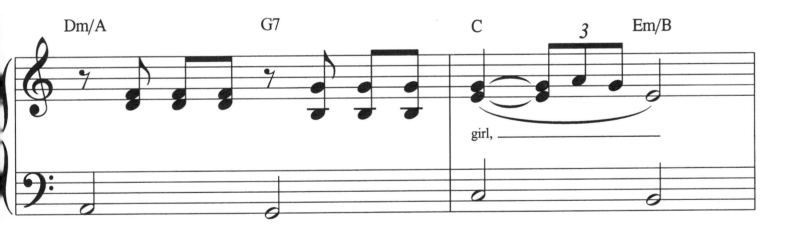

# HEY JUDE

Words and Music by JOHN LENNON
and PAUL McCARTNEY

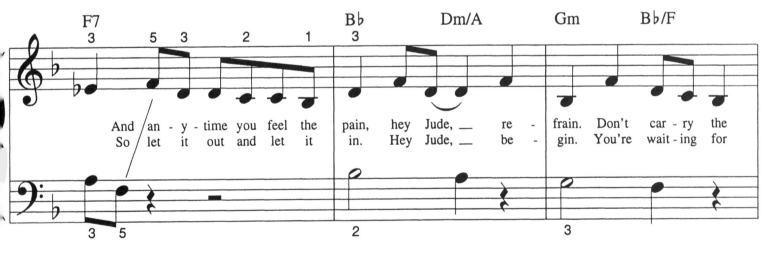

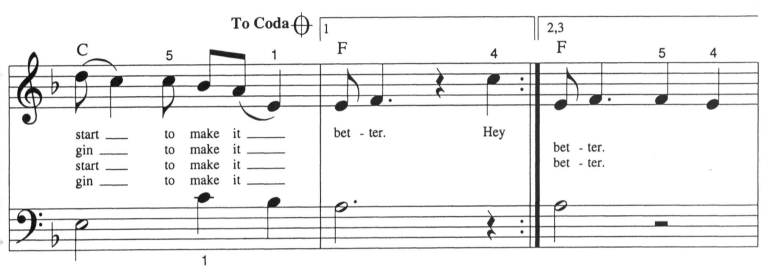

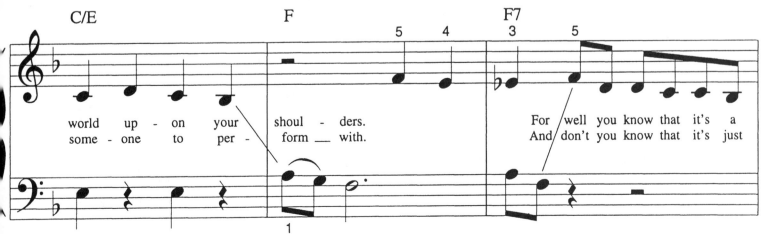

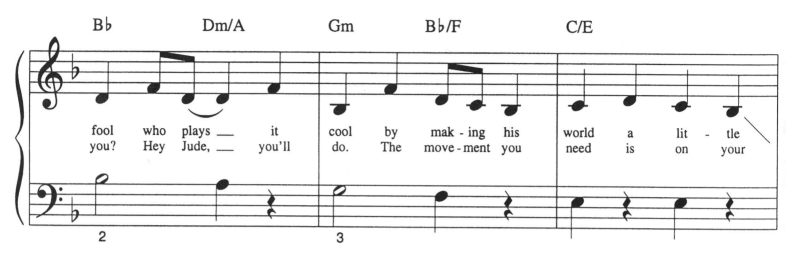

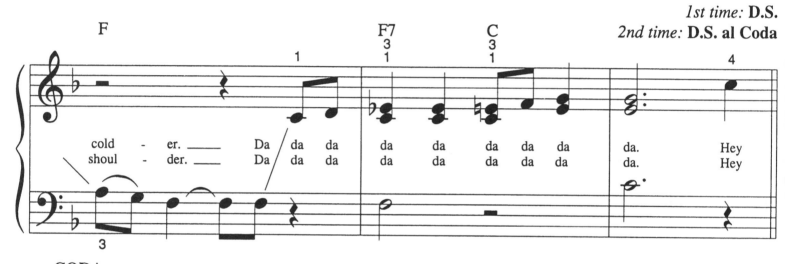

*1st time:* **D.S.**
*2nd time:* **D.S. al Coda**

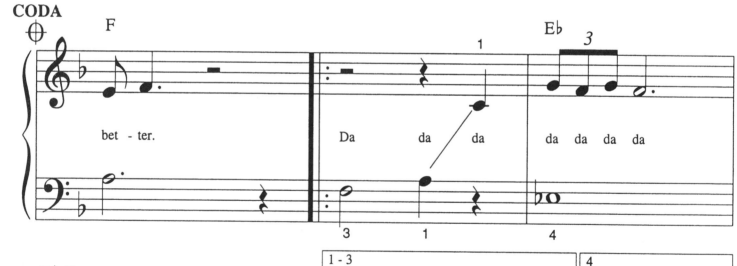

# I SAW HER STANDING THERE

Words and Music by JOHN LENNON
and PAUL McCARTNEY

Bright Rock

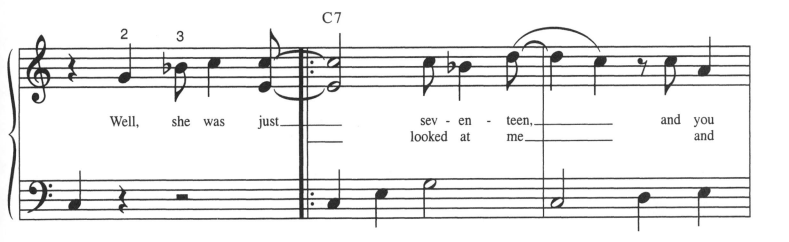

Well, she was just___ sev - en - teen,___ and you
looked at me___ and

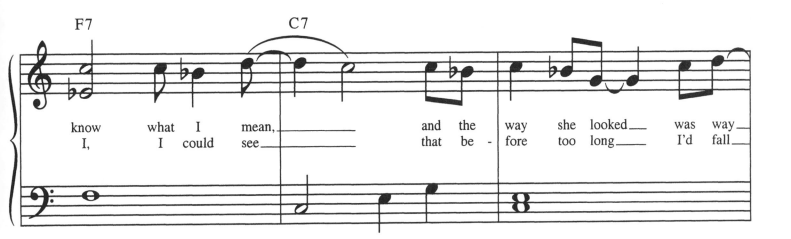

know what I mean,___ and the way she looked___ was way___
I, I could see___ that be - fore too long___ I'd fall___

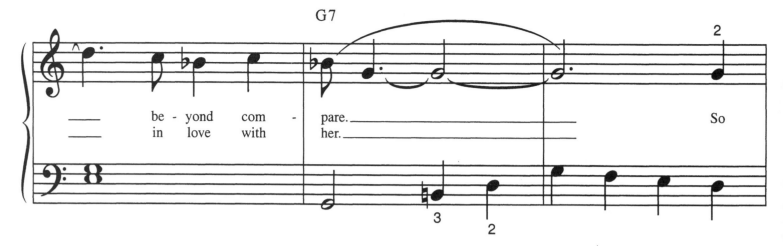

be - yond com - pare. _____ So
in love with her. _____

how could I dance ____ with an - oth - er,
She would - n't dance ____ with an - oth - er,

woo, when I saw her stand - ing
woo, when I saw her stand - ing

there. Well, she ___
there. Well, my

heart went boom___ when I crossed that room,

___ and I held her hand___ in

mi - een,___ een.___

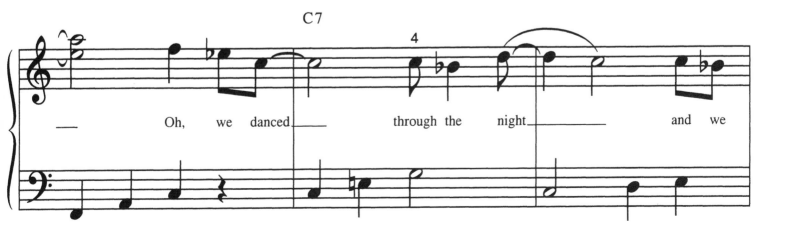

___ Oh, we danced___ through the night___ and we

held each oth - er tight, ___ ___ and be - fore too long ___ I fell ___

— in love with her. ___ Now

I'll nev - er dance ___ with an - oth - er,

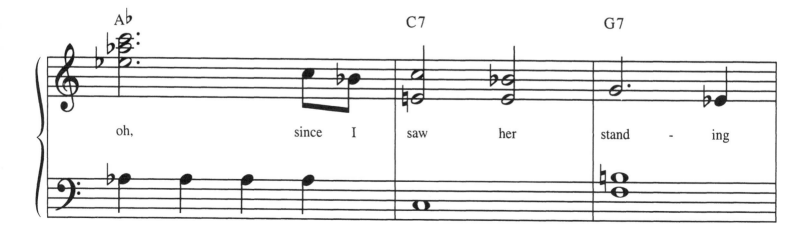

oh, since I saw her stand - ing

# I WILL

Words and Music by JOHN LENNON
and PAUL McCARTNEY

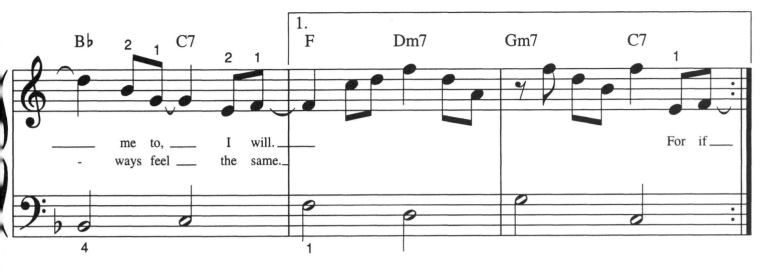

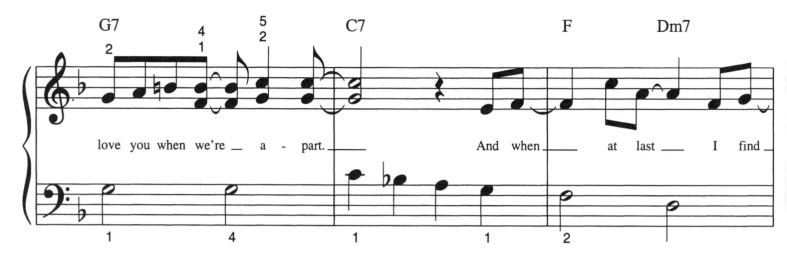

love you when we're __ a - part. ___ And when ___ at last ___ I find

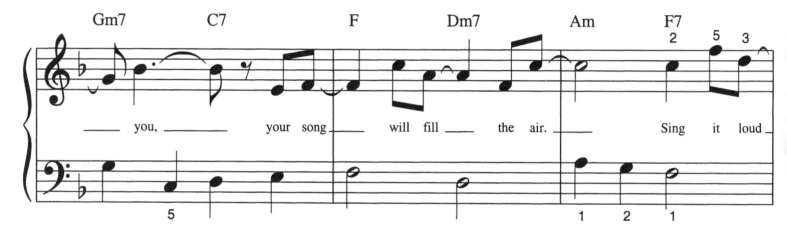

___ you, ____ your song ___ will fill ___ the air. ___ Sing it loud

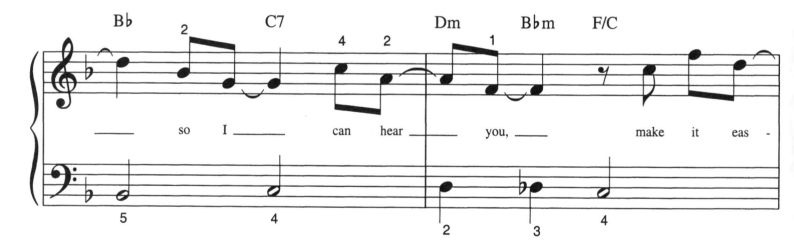

___ so I ___ can hear ___ you, ___ make it eas -

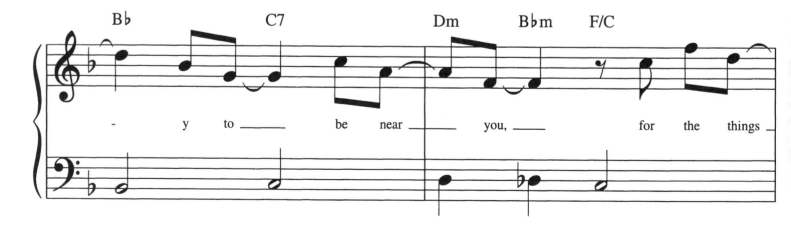

- y to ___ be near ___ you, ___ for the things

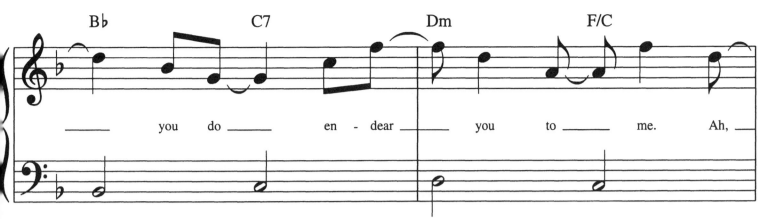

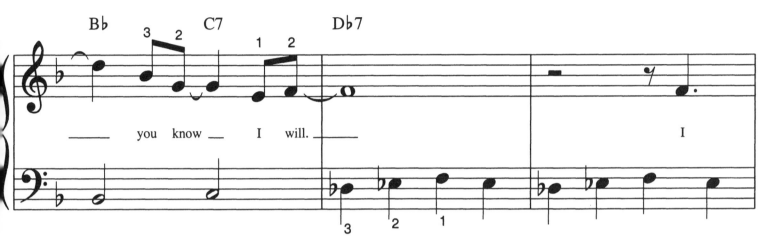

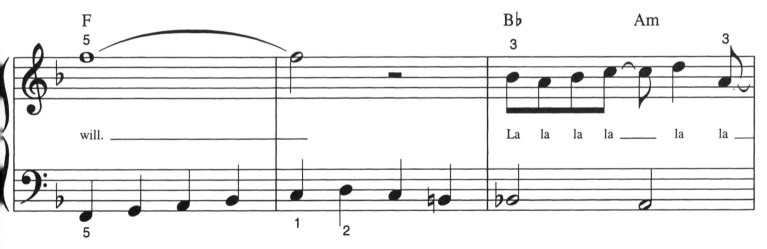

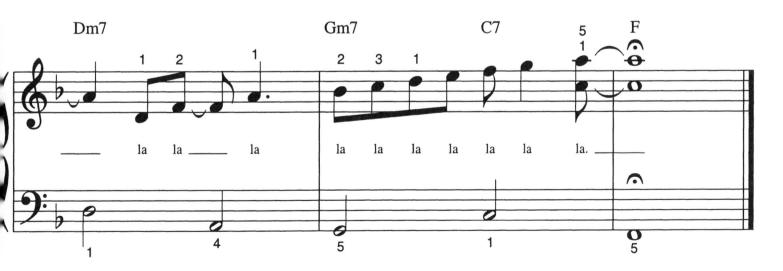

# I'LL FOLLOW THE SUN

Words and Music by JOHN LENNON
and PAUL McCARTNEY

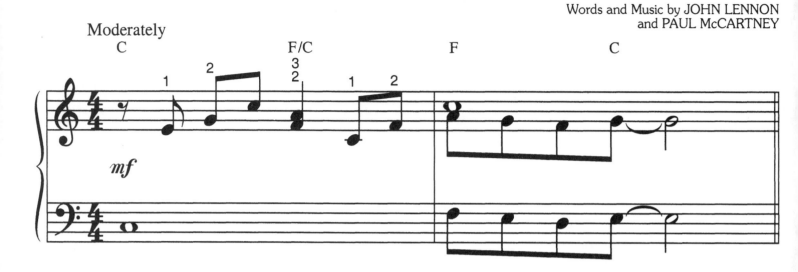

One day____ you'll look____ to see I've gone,
Some day____ you'll know____ I was the one,

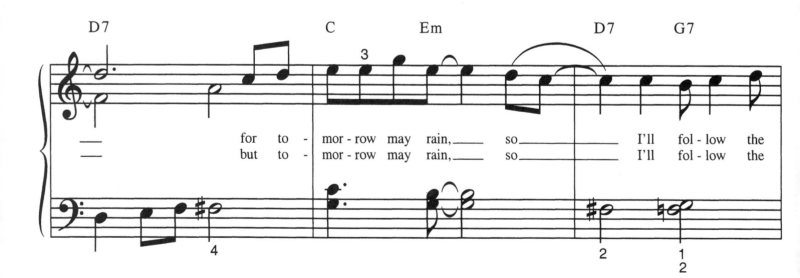

for to- mor-row may rain,____ so____ I'll fol-low the
but to- mor-row may rain,____ so____ I'll fol-low the

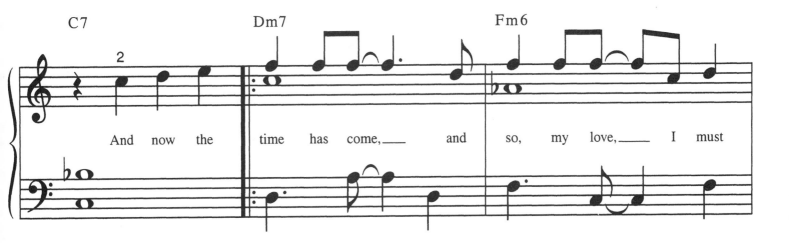

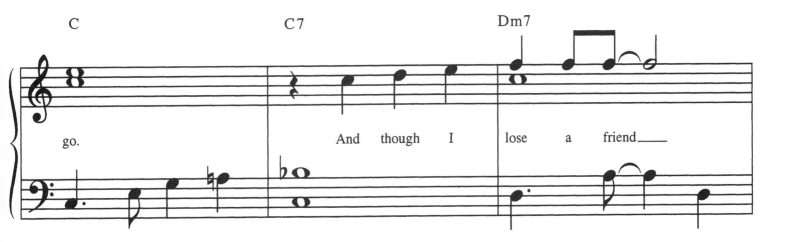

one day___ you'll find___ that I have gone,

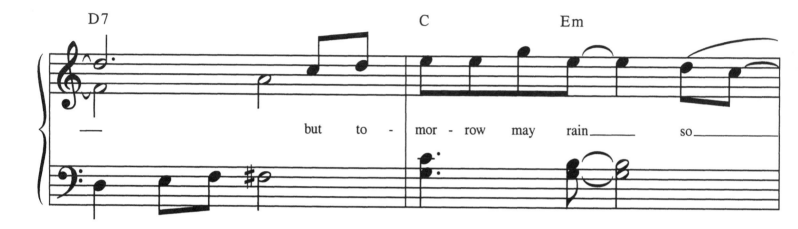

___ but to - mor - row may rain___ so___

___ I'll fol - low the sun. And now the

sun._____ *rit.*

# IF I FELL

Words and Music by JOHN LENNON
and PAUL McCARTNEY

Moderately slow

If I fell in love with you would you

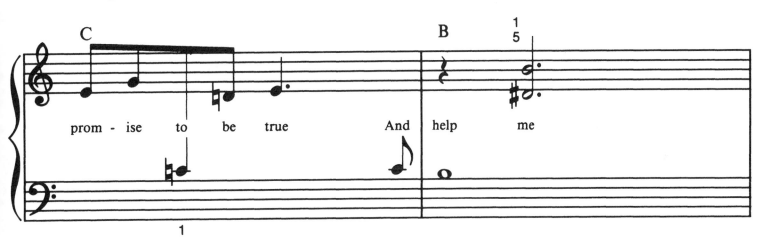

prom - ise to be true And help me

un - der - stand? 'Cause I've been in love be - fore, and I

found that love was more than just hold - ing hands. If I

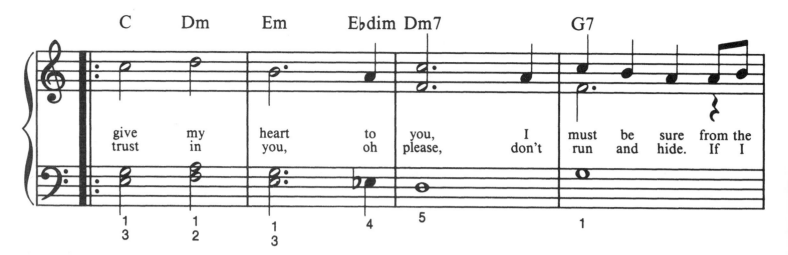

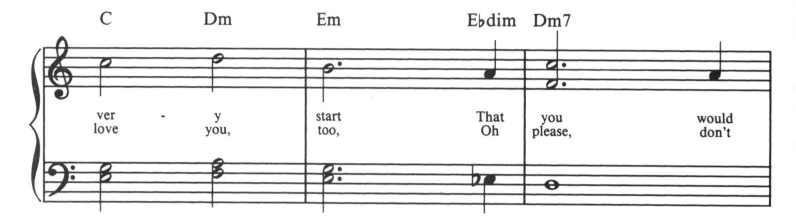

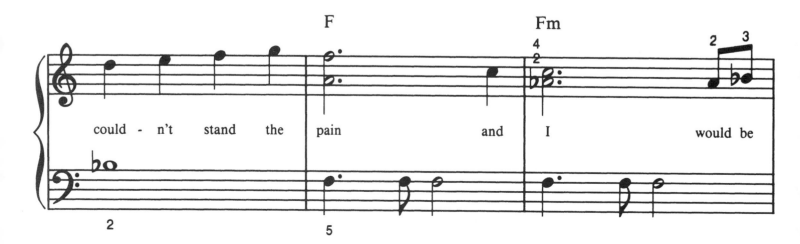

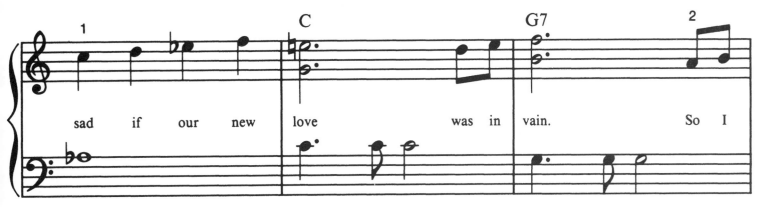

sad    if    our    new    love           was    in    vain.        So    I

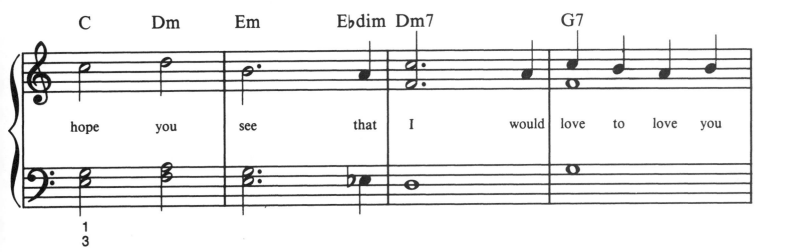

hope          you          see          that    I          would    love    to    love    you

And          that          she          will    cry          when    she    learns    we    are

two,                    if    I    fell    in    love    with          you.

5

# IN MY LIFE

Words and Music by JOHN LENNON<br>and PAUL McCARTNEY

Moderately, with expression

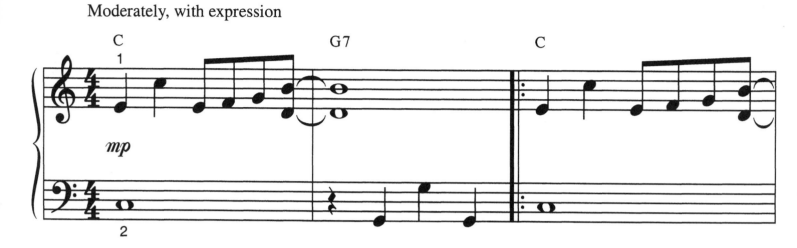

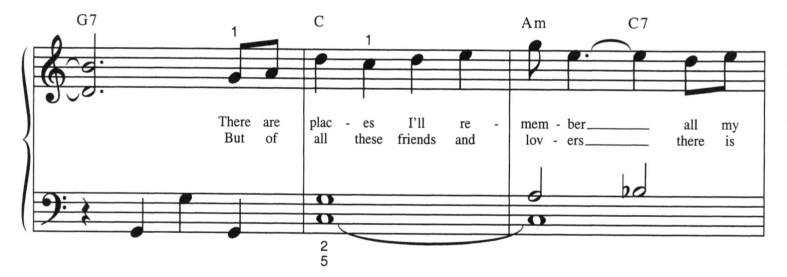

There are | plac - es I'll re - | mem - ber_____ all my
But of | all these friends and | lov - ers_____ there is

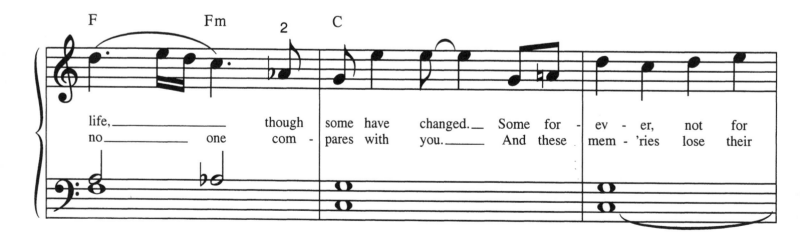

life,_____ | though | some have | changed.___ Some for - | ev - er, not for
no_____ one com - | pares with | you.___ And these | mem - 'ries lose their

better;_____ some have gone_____ and some re - main.____ All these
mean - ing_____ when I think of__ love as some - thing new.____ Tho' I

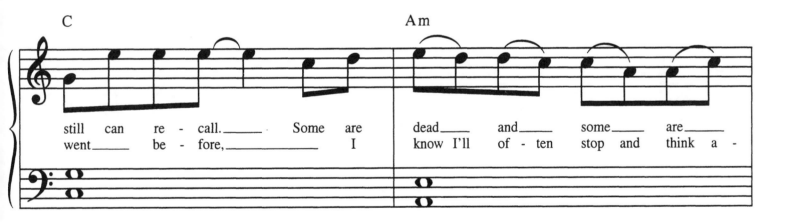

(1.) plac - es____ had____ their____ mo - ments_____ with lov - ers and friends____ I
(2., 3.) know__ I'll__ nev - er lose af - fec - tion_____ for peo - ple and things____ that

still can re - call.____ Some are dead____ and____ some____ are_____
went____ be - fore,_____ I know I'll of - ten stop and think a -

liv - ing,_____ in my_____ life I've loved them all.____
bout them,_____ in my_____ life I love you more.____

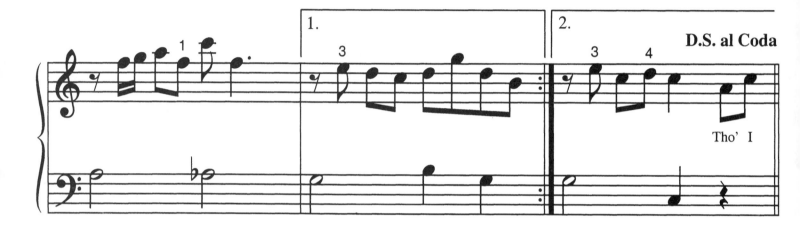

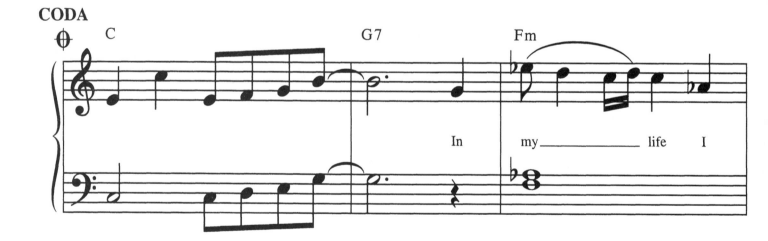

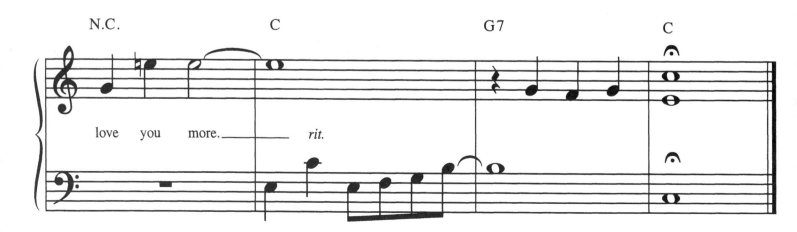

# LUCY IN THE SKY WITH DIAMONDS

Words and Music by JOHN LENNON
and PAUL McCARTNEY

48

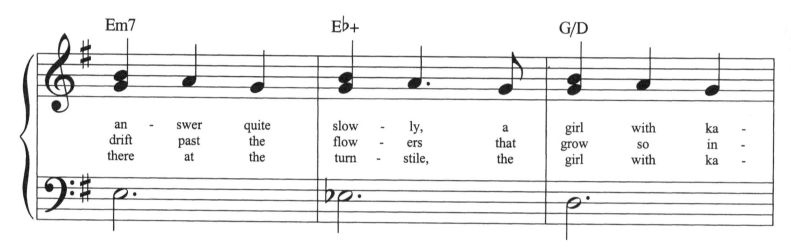

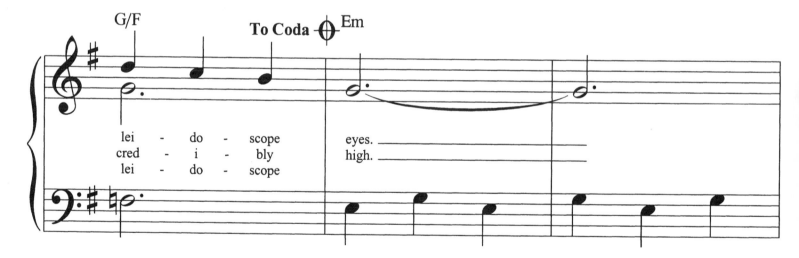

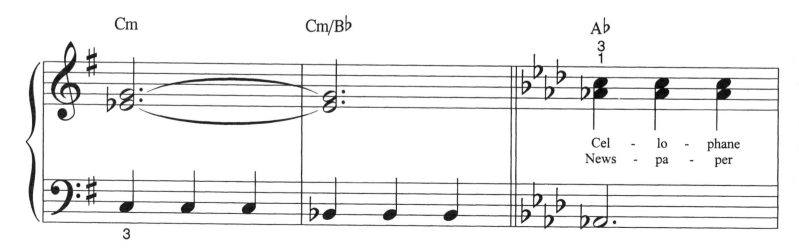

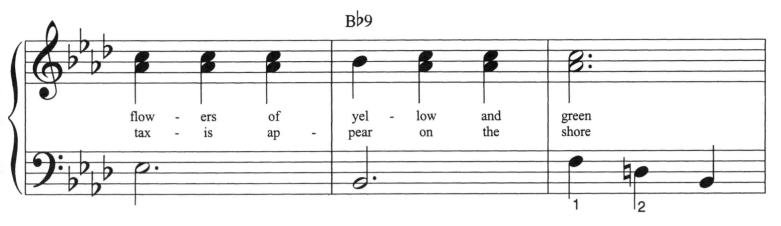

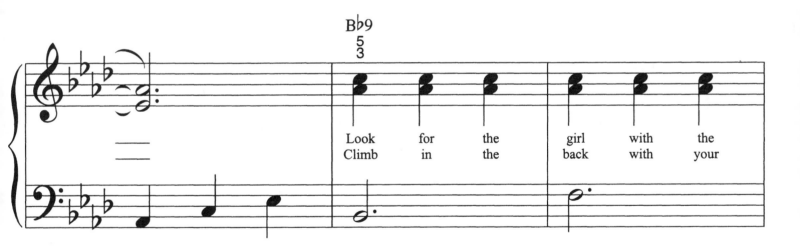

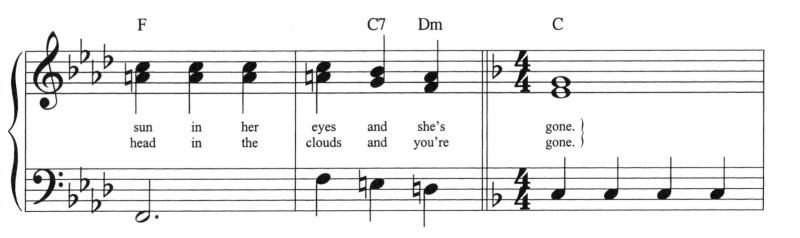

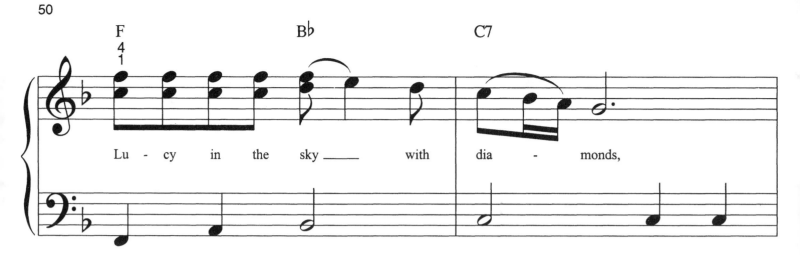

Lu - cy in the sky ____ with dia - monds,

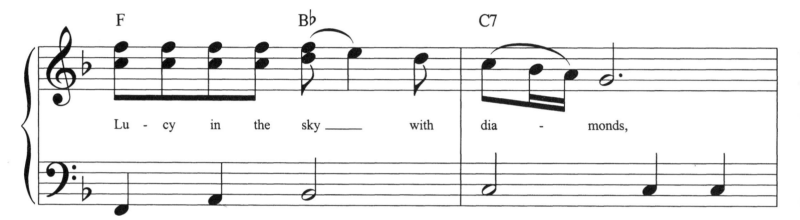

Lu - cy in the sky ____ with dia - monds,

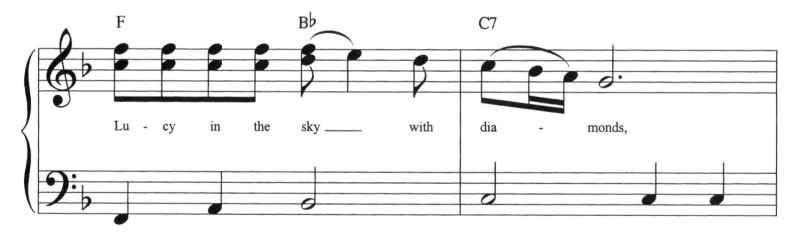

Lu - cy in the sky ____ with dia - monds,

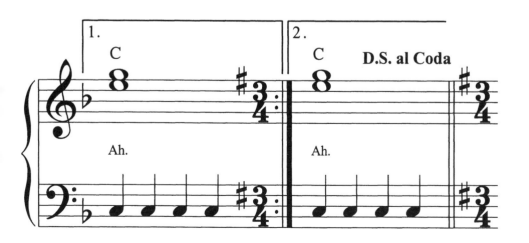

1. Ah.

2. **D.S. al Coda** Ah.

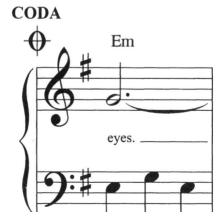

**CODA**

eyes. ____

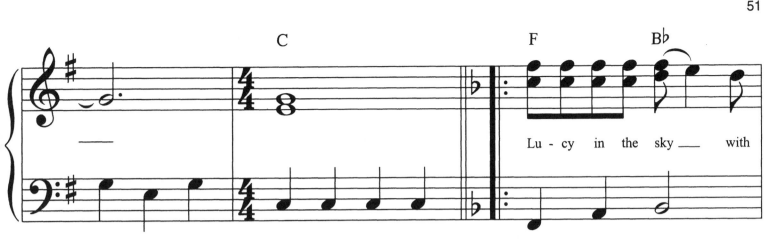

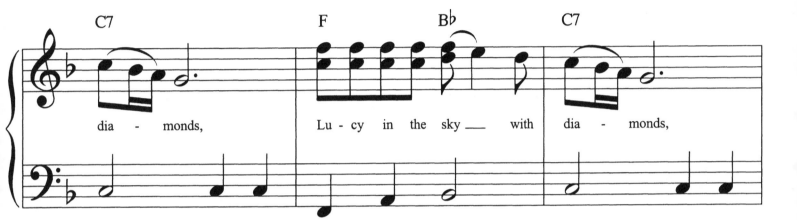

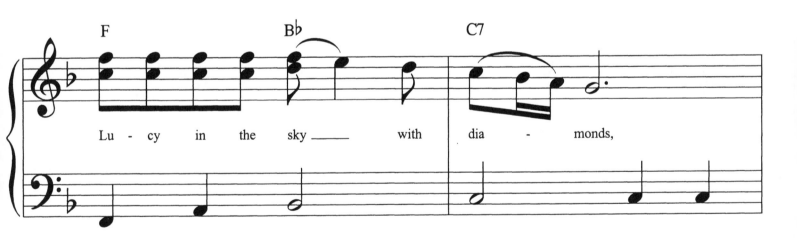

C          G

Ah.

# LADY MADONNA

Words and Music by JOHN LENNON
and PAUL McCARTNEY

Brightly, with a beat

Lady Madonna, children at your feet,
Lady Madonna, baby at your breast,
Lady Madonna, lying on the bed,

wonder how you manage to make
wonders how you manage to feed
listen to the music playing

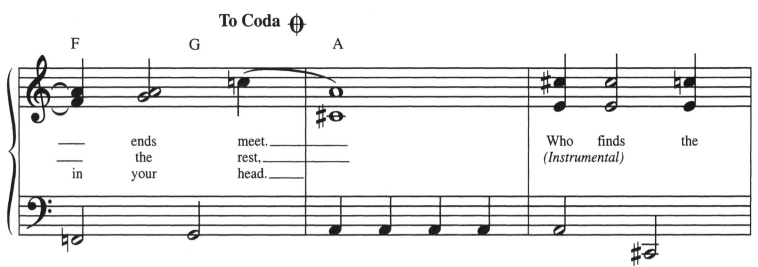

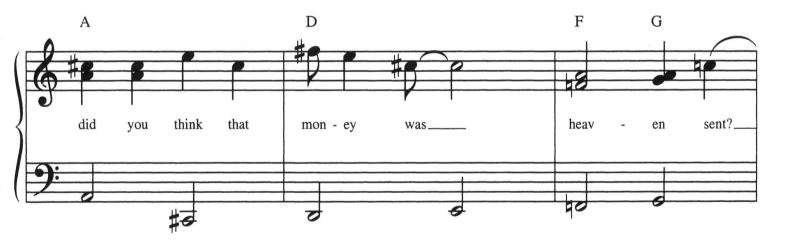

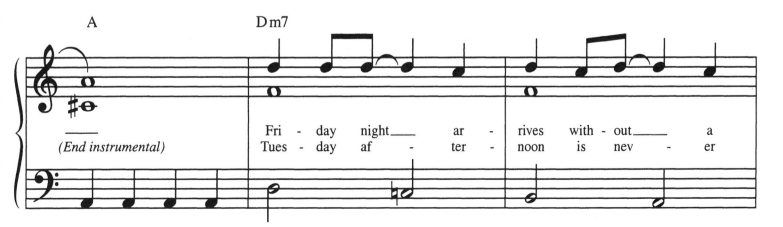

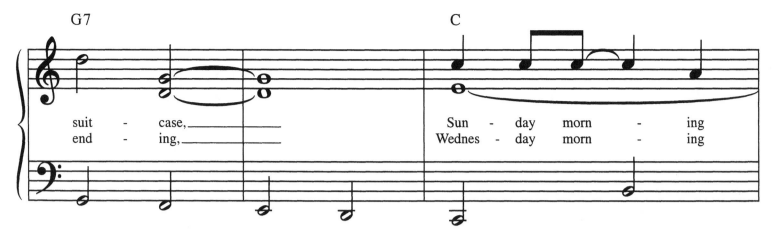

suit - case,_____
end - ing,_____

Sun - day morn - ing
Wednes - day morn - ing

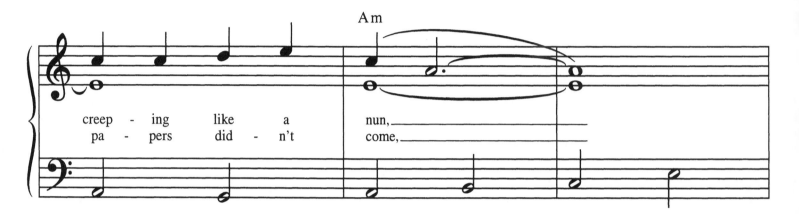

creep - ing like a
pa - pers did - n't

nun,_____
come,_____

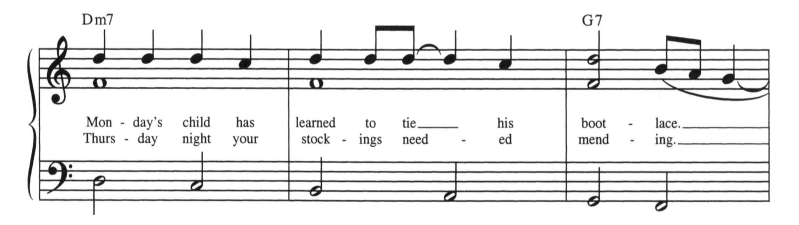

Mon - day's child has
Thurs - day night your

learned to tie_____ his
stock - ings need - ed

boot - lace._____
mend - ing._____

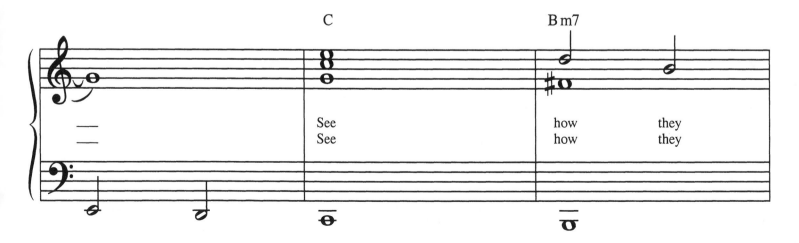

_____
_____

See
See

how they
how they

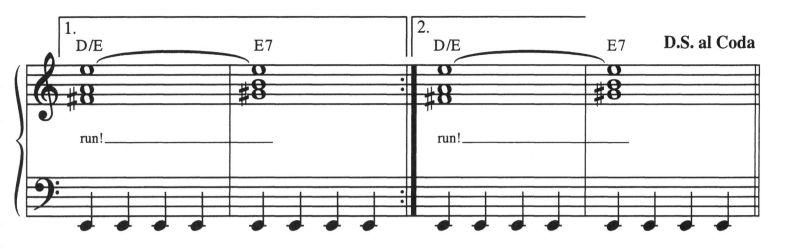

D.S. al Coda

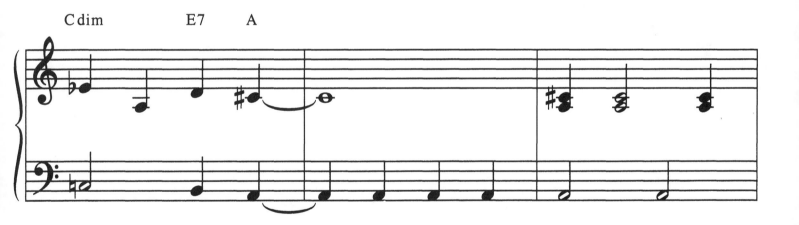

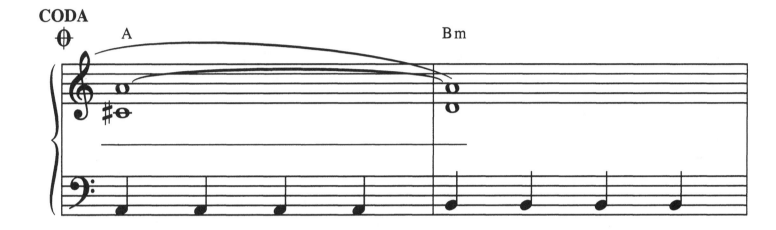

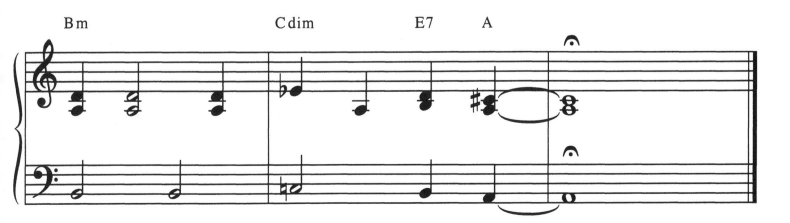

# LET IT BE

Words and Music by JOHN LENNON
and PAUL McCARTNEY

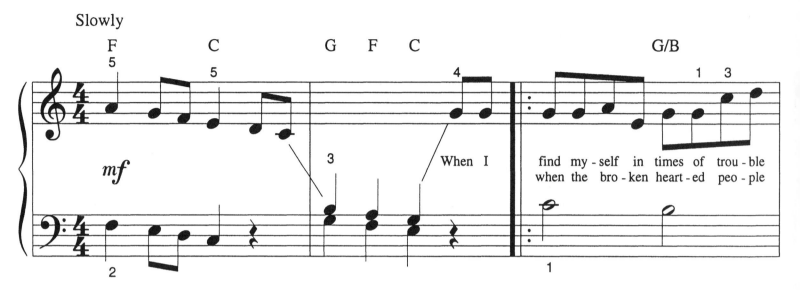

When I / find my-self in times of trou-ble / when the bro-ken heart-ed peo-ple

Moth-er Mar-y comes to me, / speak-ing words of wis-dom. Let it / be. / And
liv-ing in the world a-gree, / there will be an an-swer. Let it / be. / For

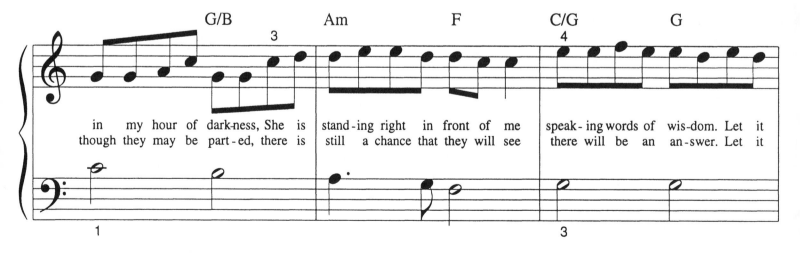

in my hour of dark-ness, She is / stand-ing right in front of me / speak-ing words of wis-dom. Let it
though they may be part-ed, there is / still a chance that they will see / there will be an an-swer. Let it

# PENNY LANE

Words and Music by JOHN LENNON
and PAUL McCARTNEY

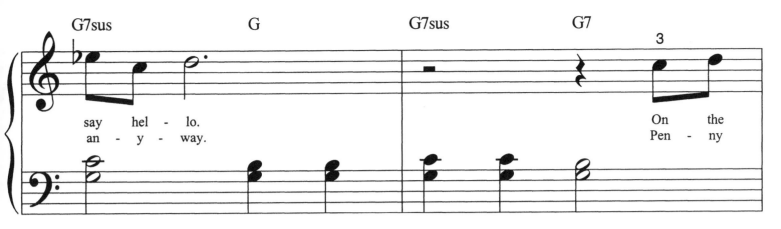

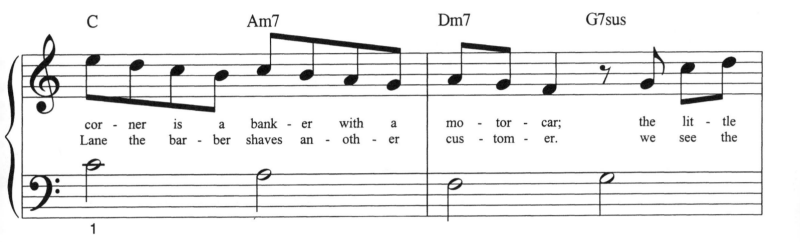

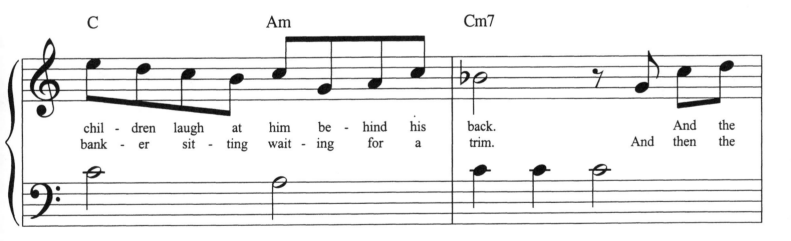

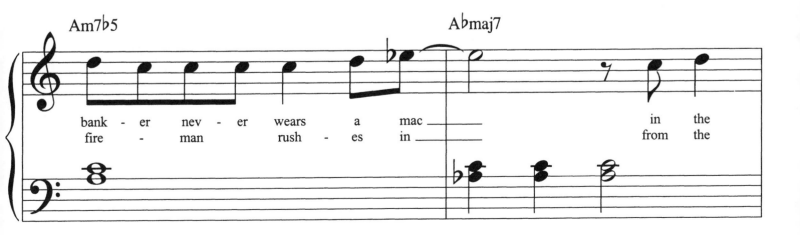

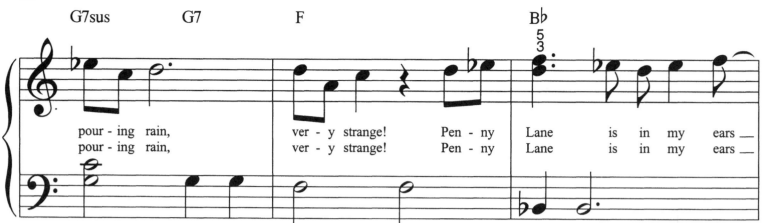

pour - ing rain, ver - y strange! Pen - ny Lane is in my ears __
pour - ing rain, ver - y strange! Pen - ny Lane is in my ears __

__ and in my eyes, __
__ and in my eyes, __

wet be - neath the blue __ sub - ur - ban skies __ I sit. And
there be - neath the blue __ sub - ur - ban skies __ I sit. And

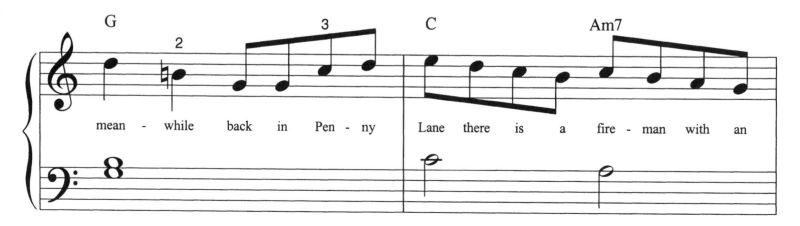

mean - while back in Pen - ny Lane there is a fire - man with an

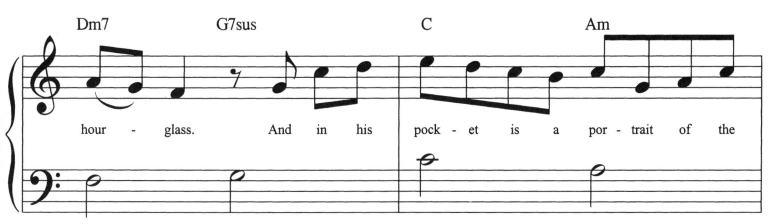

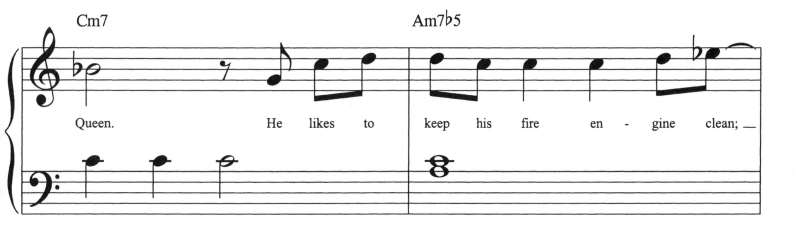

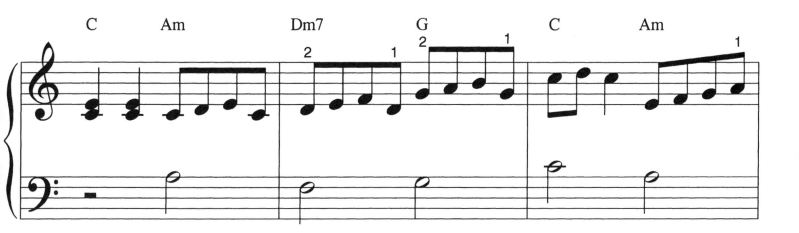

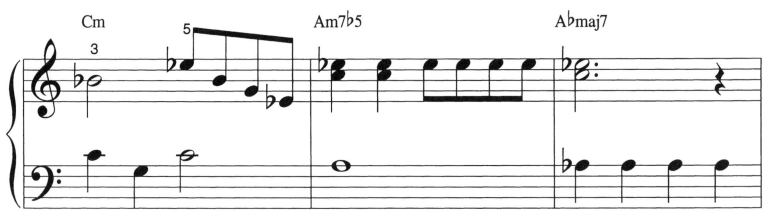

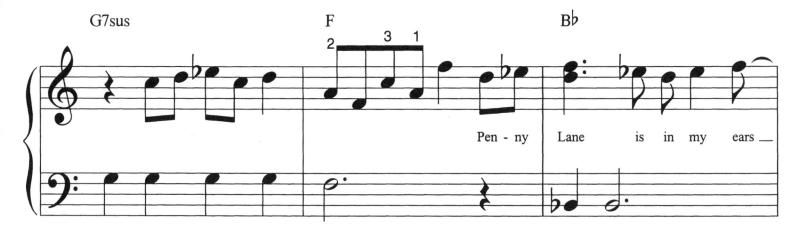

Pen - ny Lane is in my ears ___

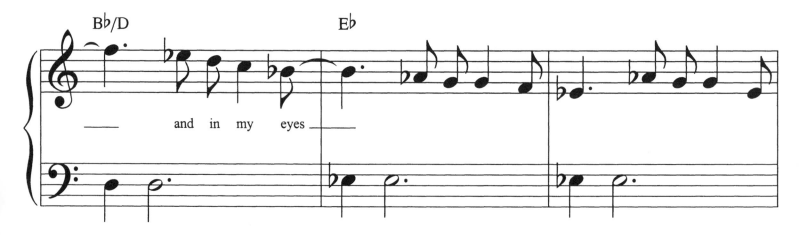

___ and in my eyes ___

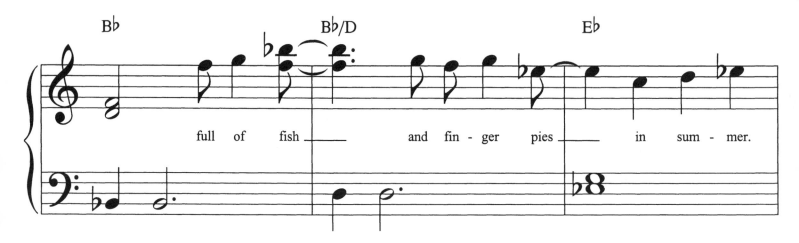

full of fish ___ and fin - ger pies ___ in sum - mer.

D.S. al Coda

**CODA**

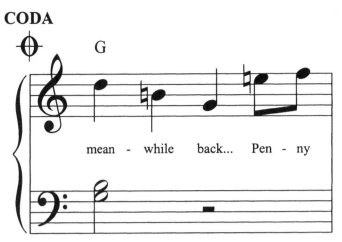

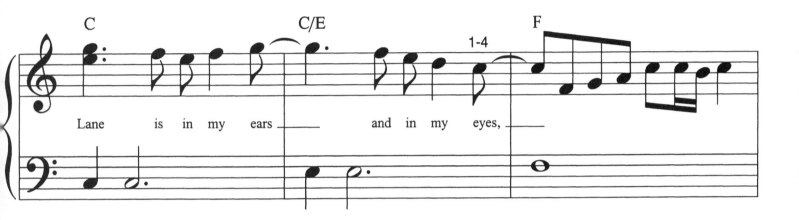

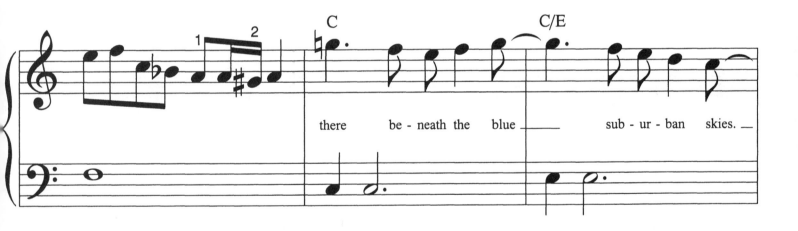

# PLEASE PLEASE ME

Words and Music by JOHN LENNON
and PAUL McCARTNEY

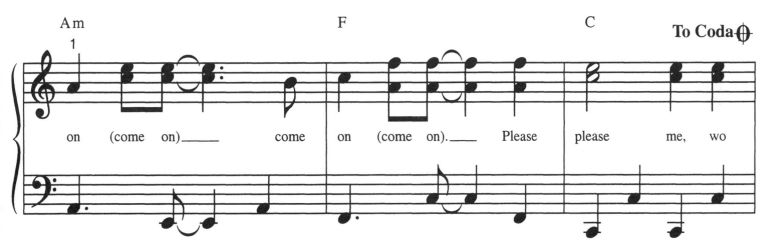

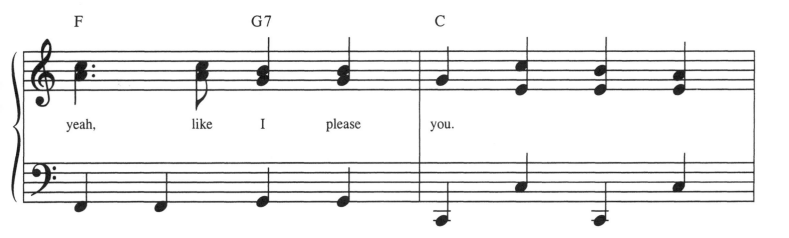

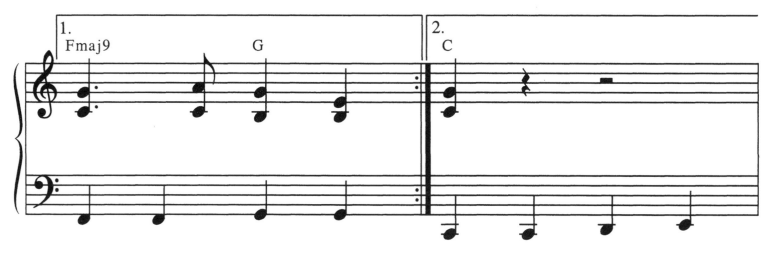

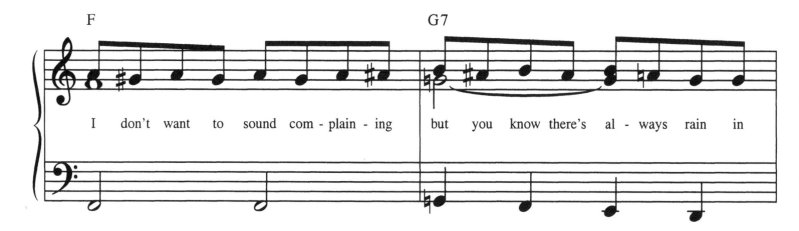

I don't want to sound com - plain - ing but you know there's al - ways rain in

my_____ heart. (in_____ my heart).

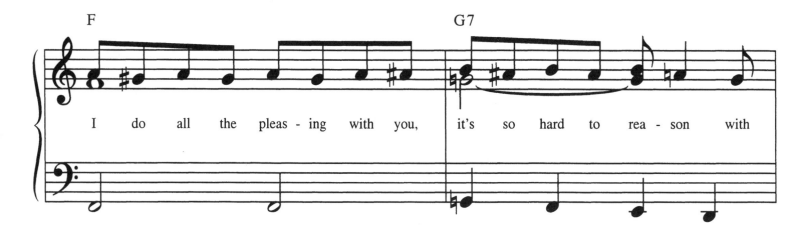

I do all the pleas - ing with you, it's so hard to rea - son with

you, wo yeah, why do you make me

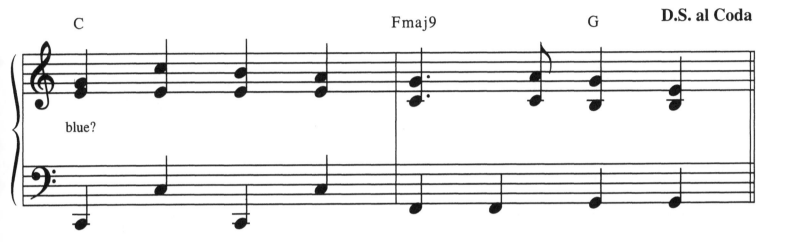

**D.S. al Coda**

blue?

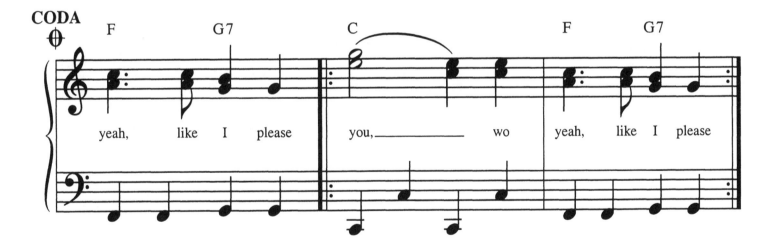

**CODA**

yeah, like I please you, wo yeah, like I please

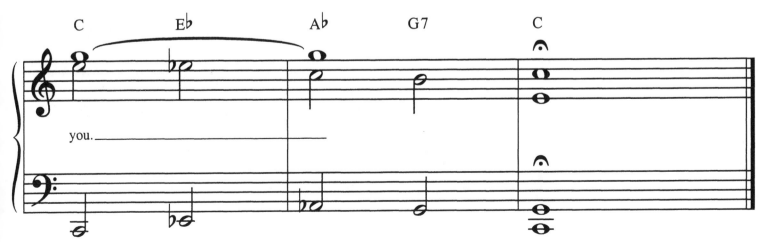

you.

# REVOLUTION

Words and Music by JOHN LENNON
and PAUL McCARTNEY

Moderate Rock Shuffle

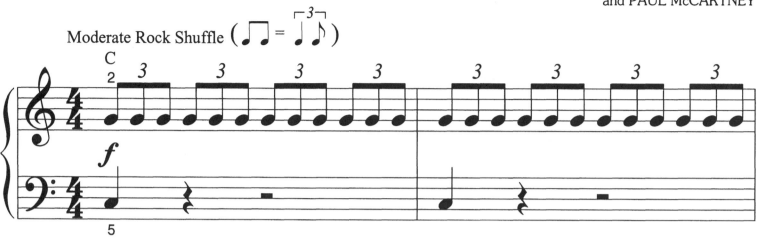

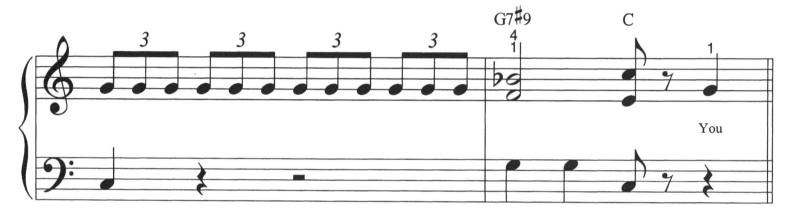

say you want a rev-o - lu - tion, _____ well
say you got a real so - lu - tion, _____ well
say you'll change the con - sti - tu - tion, _____ well

You

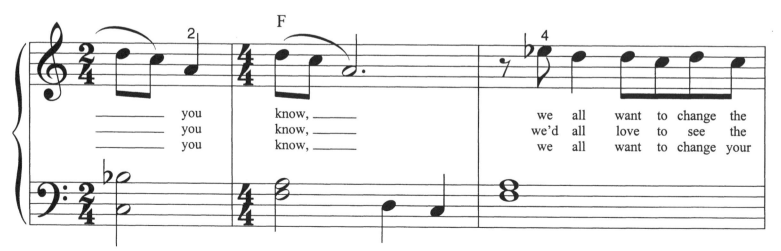

_____ you know, _____
_____ you know, _____
_____ you know, _____

we all want to change the
we'd all love to see the
we all want to change your

world. _____
plan. _____
head. _____

You tell me that it's e - vo -
You ask me for a con - tri -
You tell me it's the in - sti -

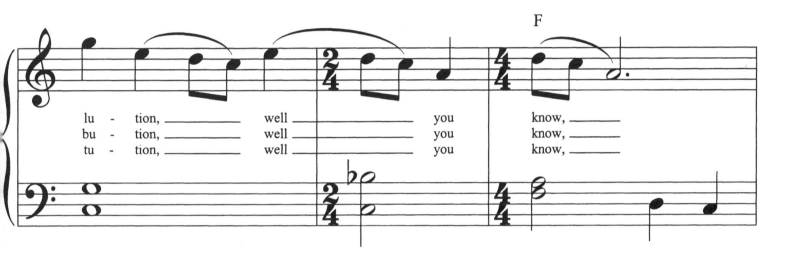

lu - tion, _____ well _____ you know, _____
bu - tion, _____ well _____ you know, _____
tu - tion, _____ well _____ you know, _____

we all want to change the world. _____
we're all do - ing what we can. _____
you bet - ter free your mind in - stead. _____

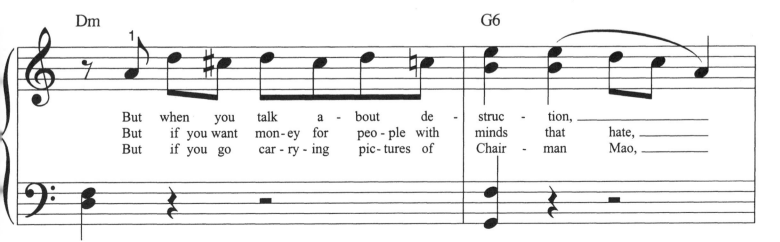

But when you talk a - bout de - struc - tion, _____
But if you want mon - ey for peo - ple with minds that hate, _____
But if you go car - ry - ing pic - tures of Chair - man Mao, _____

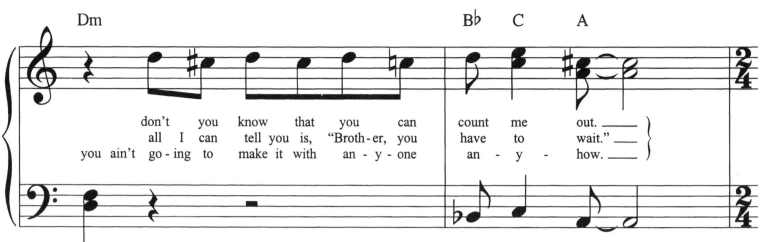

don't you know that you can count me out. _____
all I can tell you is, "Broth-er, you have to wait." _____
you ain't go-ing to make it with an-y-one an-y-how. _____

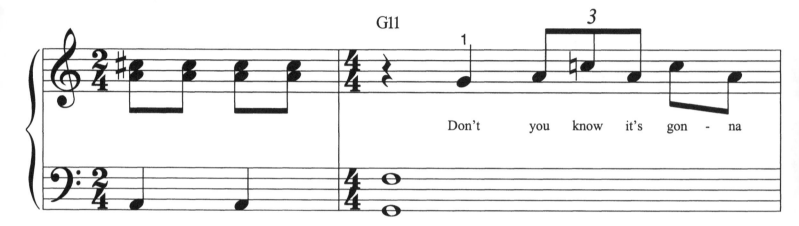

Don't you know it's gon-na

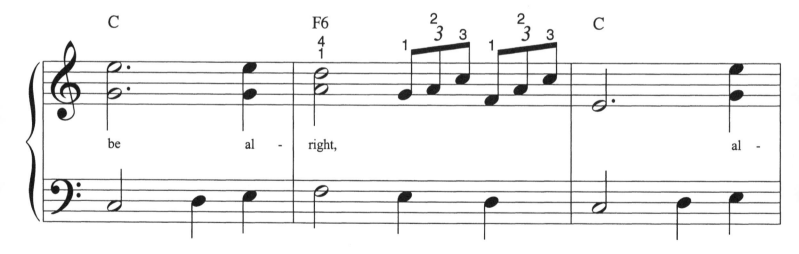

be al - right, al -

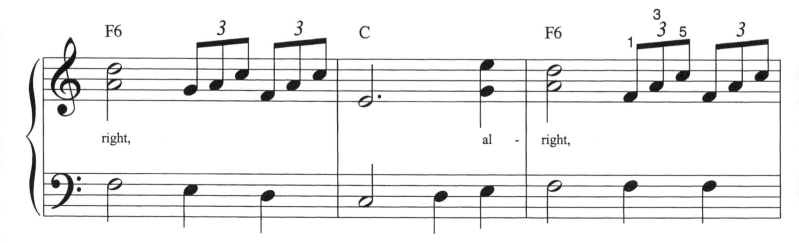

right, al - right,

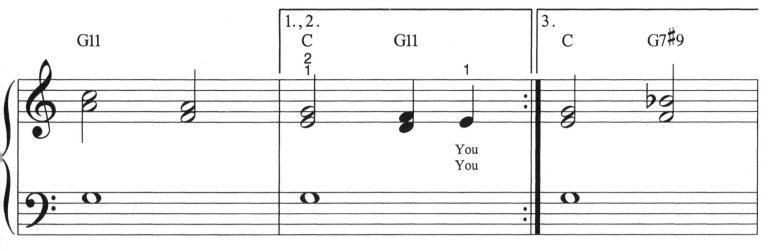

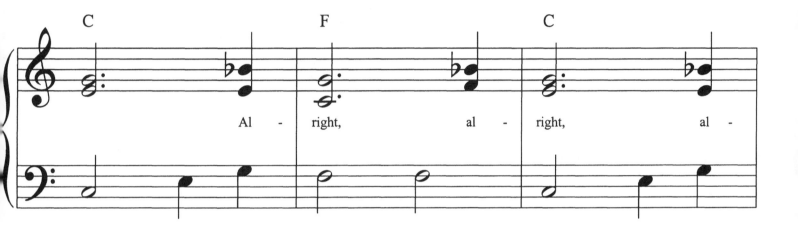

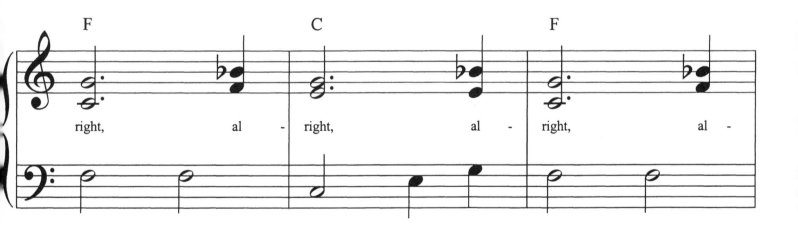

# SGT. PEPPER'S LONELY HEARTS CLUB BAND

Words and Music by JOHN LENNON
and PAUL McCARTNEY

Moderately slow, with a strong beat

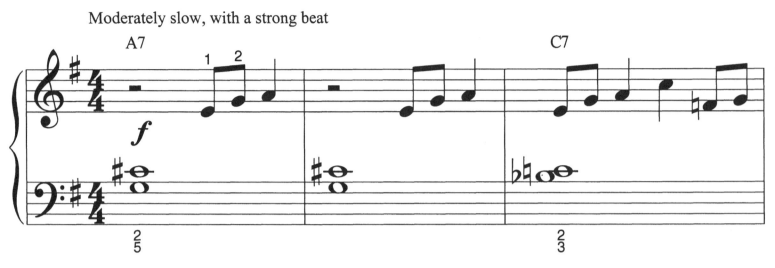

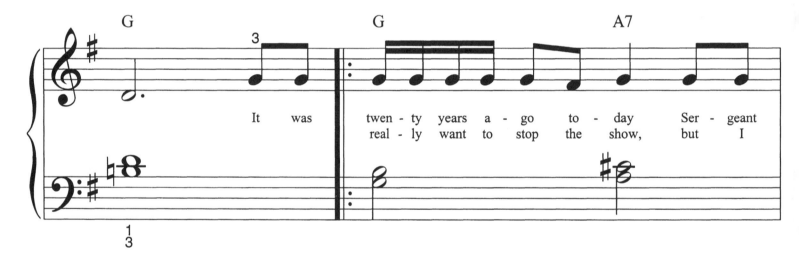

It was twenty years a-go to-day, Ser-geant
real-ly want to stop the show, but I

Pep-per taught the band to play. They've been
thought you might like to know that the

go-ing in and out of style, but they're
sing-er's going to sing a song, and he

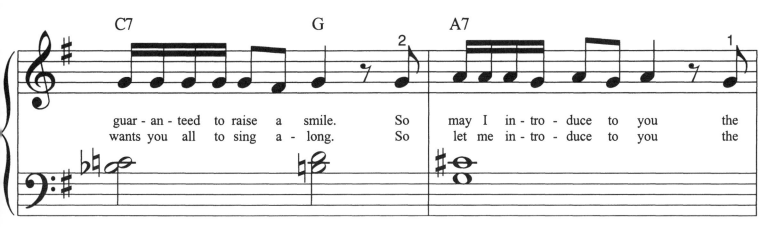

guar - an - teed to raise a smile. So
wants you all to sing a - long. So

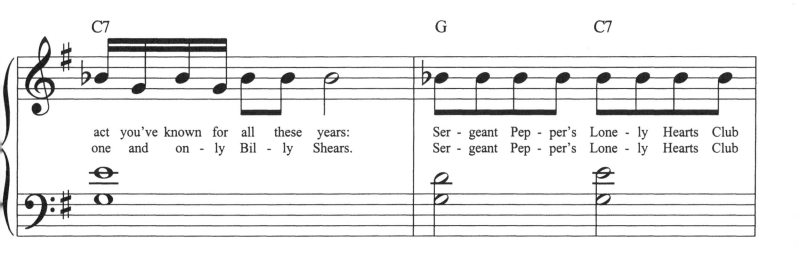

act you've known for all these years:
one and on - ly Bil - ly Shears.

Ser - geant Pep - per's Lone - ly Hearts Club
Ser - geant Pep - per's Lone - ly Hearts Club

Band. _____
Band. _____

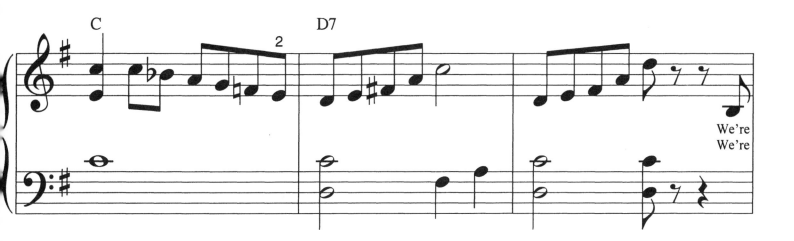

We're
We're

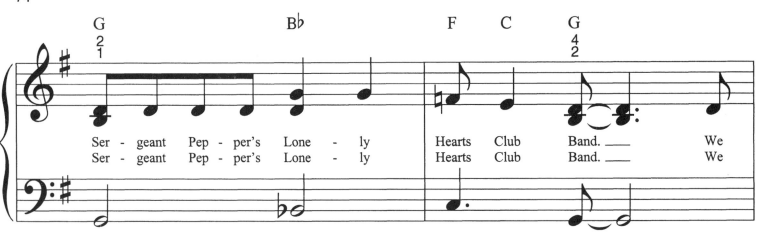

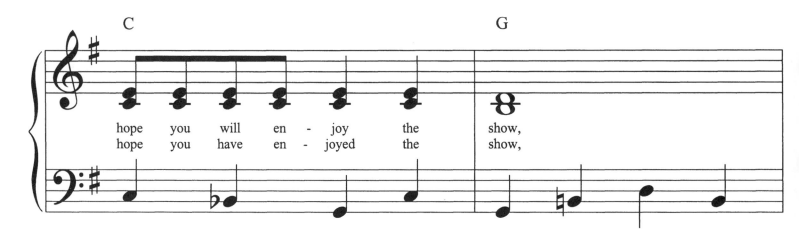

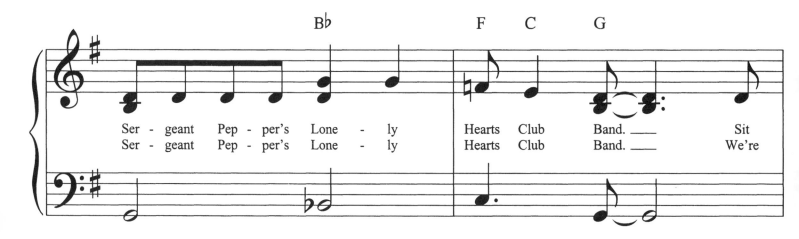

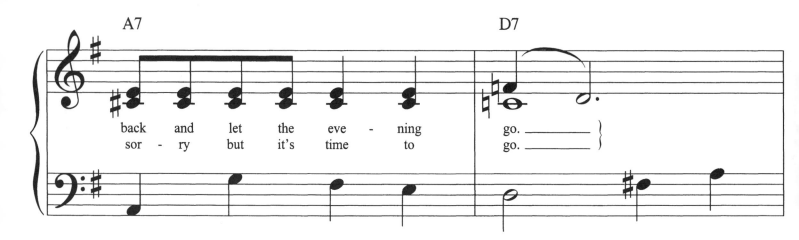

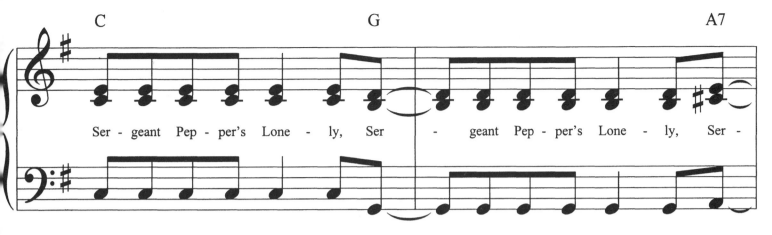

C       G       A7

Ser - geant Pep - per's Lone - ly, Ser - geant Pep - per's Lone - ly, Ser -

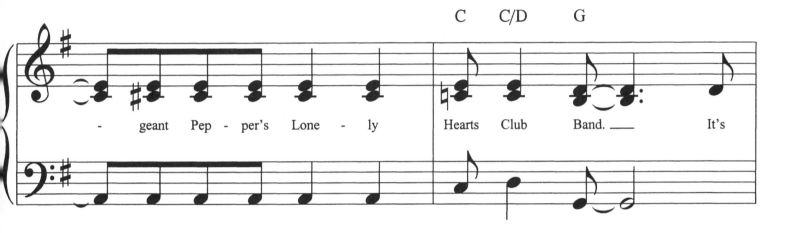

C   C/D   G

- geant Pep - per's Lone - ly    Hearts Club Band. ___ It's

1.

C       F7

won - der - ful to be here. It's cer - tain - ly a thrill. You're

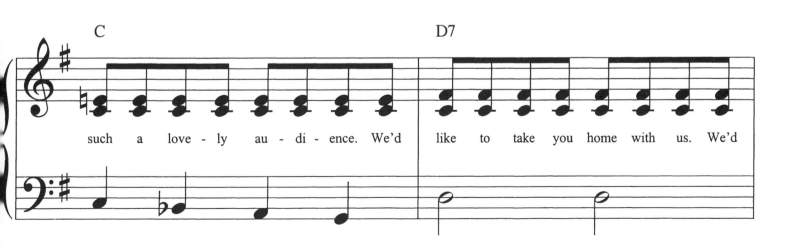

C       D7

such a love - ly au - di - ence. We'd like to take you home with us. We'd

love to take you home. I don't

2.
G                    Bb

Ser - geant Pep - per's Lone - ly

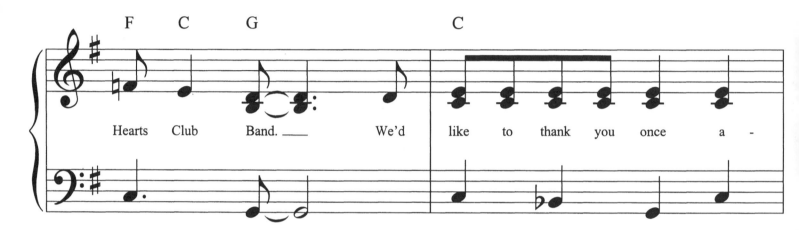

F  C  G              C

Hearts Club Band. ___ We'd like to thank you once a -

G

gain.

Bb

Ser - geant Pep - per's one and on - ly

C              G        A7

Lone - ly Hearts Club Band. It's get - ting ver - y near the

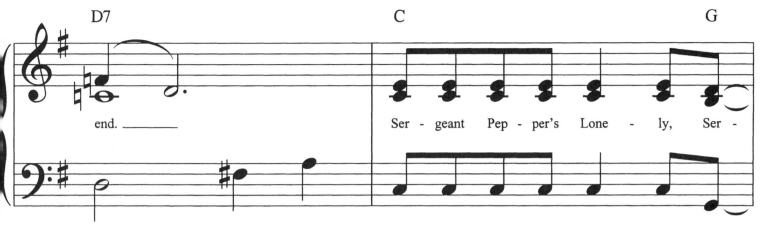

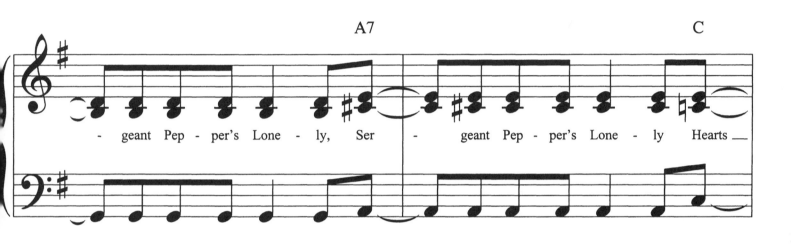

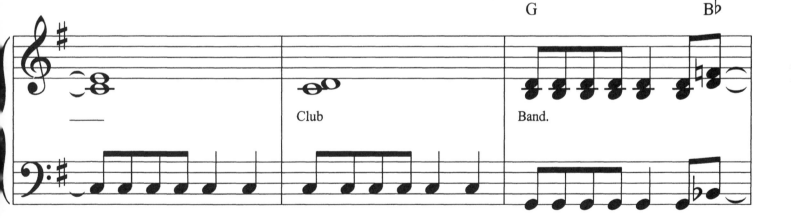

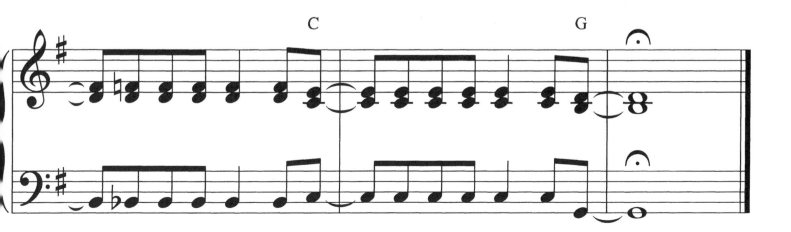

# SHE LOVES YOU

Words and Music by JOHN LENNON
and PAUL McCARTNEY

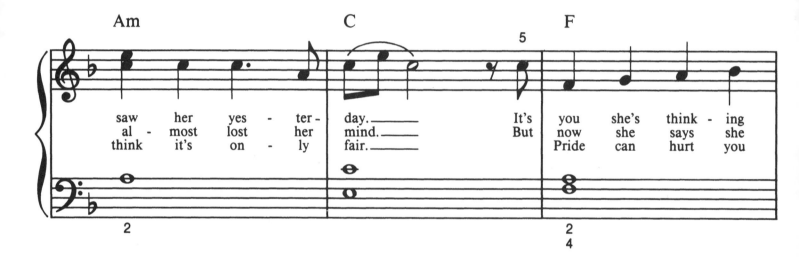

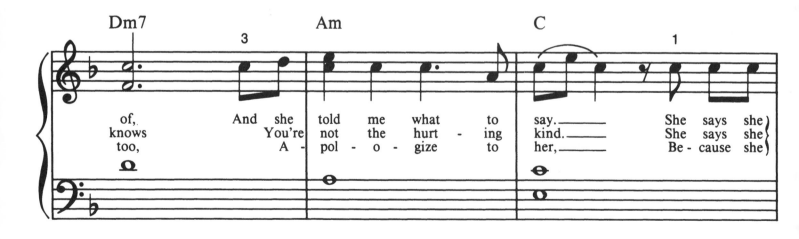

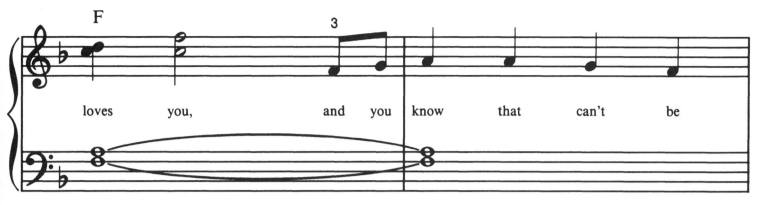

loves you, and you know that can't be

bad; Yes, she loves you and you

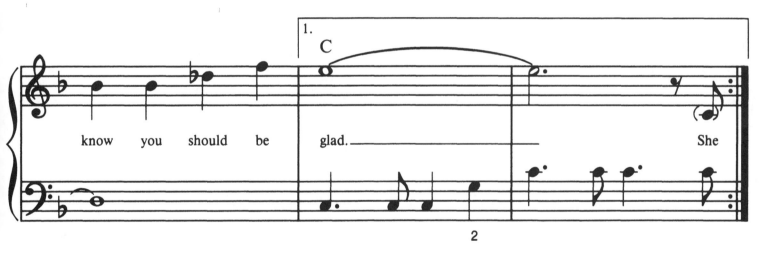

know you should be glad. She

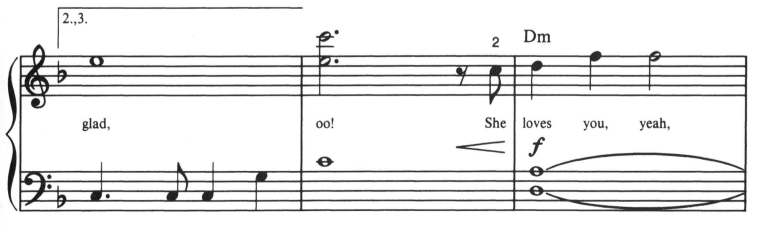

glad, oo! She loves you, yeah,

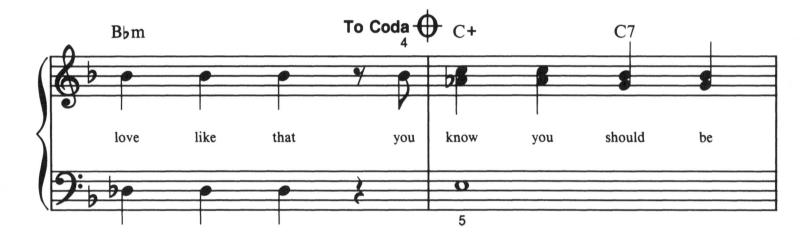

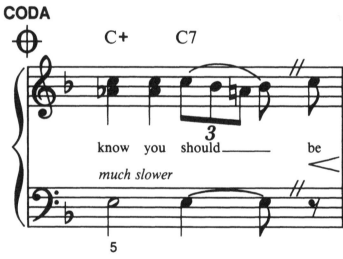

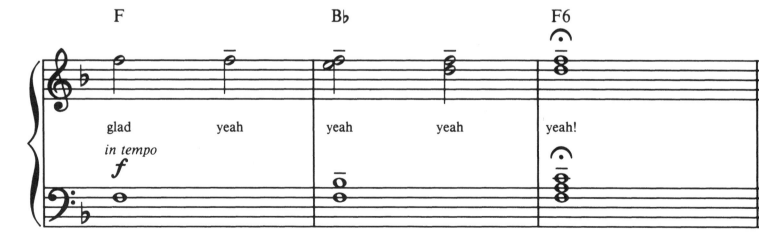

# TELL ME WHY

Words and Music by JOHN LENNON
and PAUL McCARTNEY

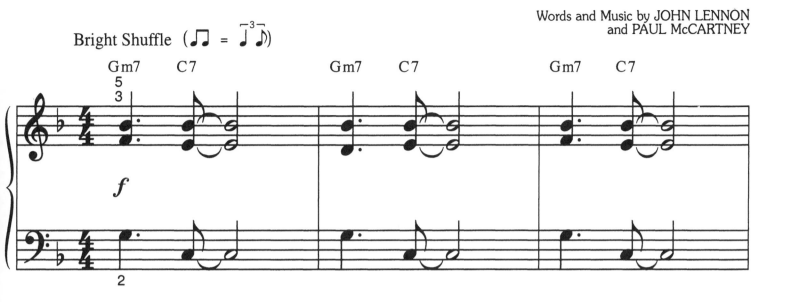

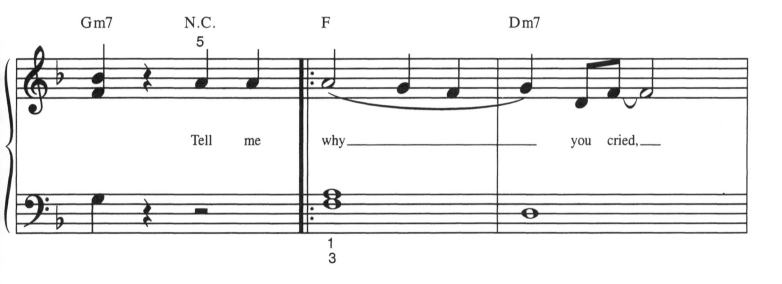

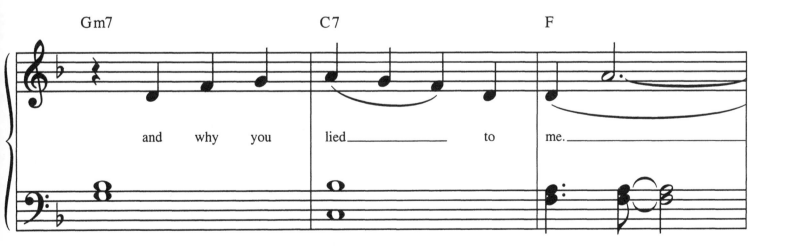

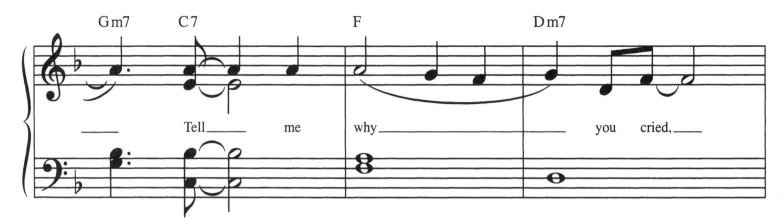

Tell_____ me why_____ you cried,_____

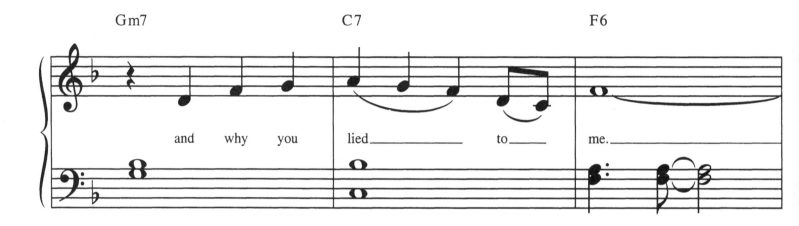

and why you lied_____ to_____ me.

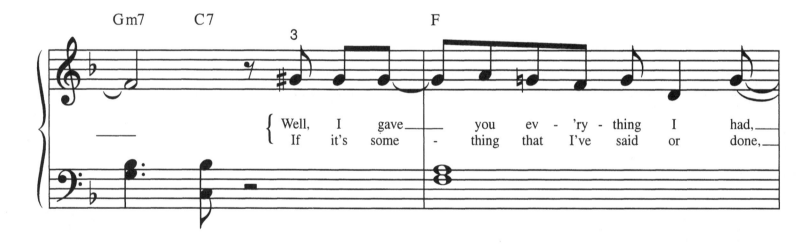

Well, I gave_____ you ev - 'ry - thing I had,
If it's some - thing that I've said or done,

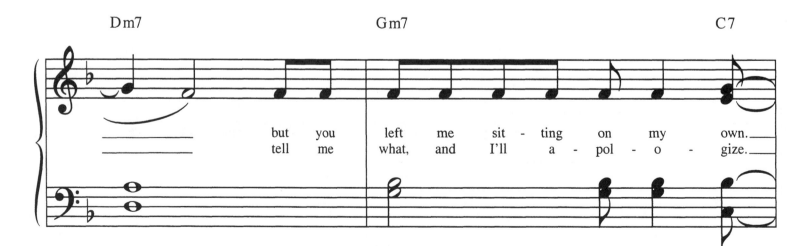

but you left me sit - ting on my own.
tell me what, and I'll a - pol - o - gize.

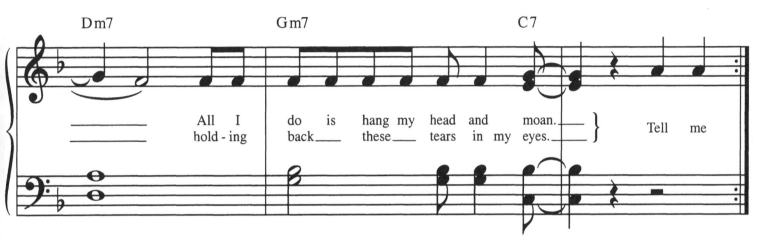

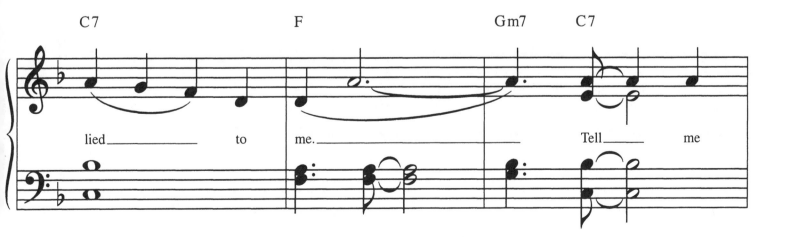

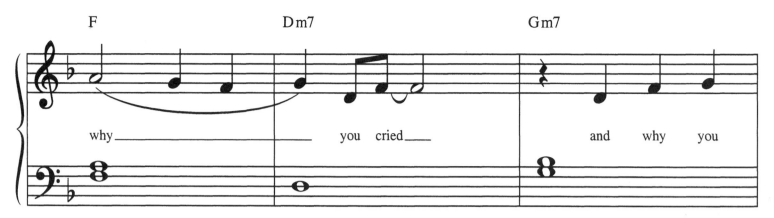

why _____ you cried ____ and why you

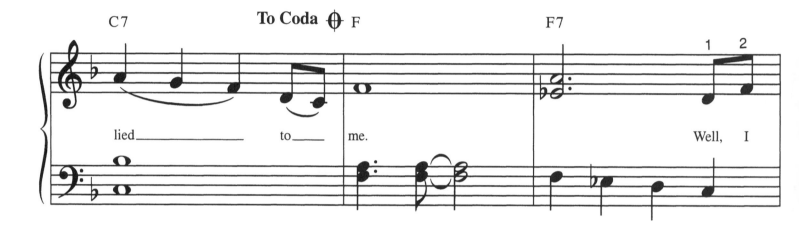

lied _____ to ____ me. Well, I

beg you on my bend-ed knees, ____ if you'll on-ly lis-ten to my pleas.

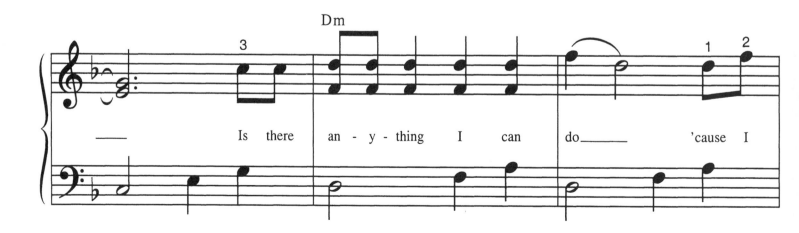

____ Is there an-y-thing I can do _____ 'cause I

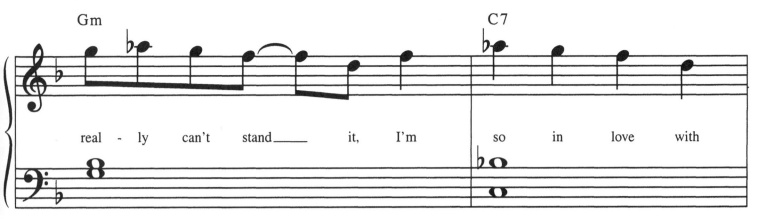

**Gm** **C7**

real - ly can't stand___ it, I'm so in love with

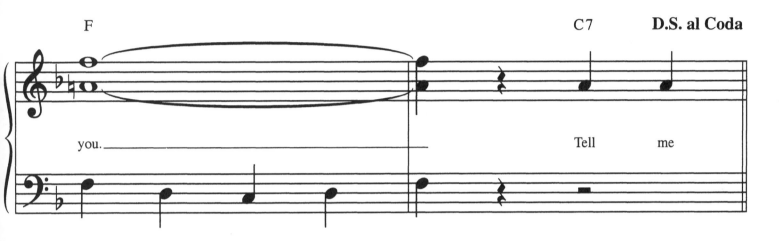

**F** **C7** **D.S. al Coda**

you.___ Tell me

 **CODA**

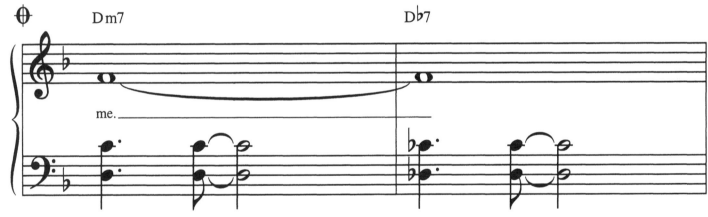

**Dm7** **Db7**

me.___

**C7sus** **C7** **F**

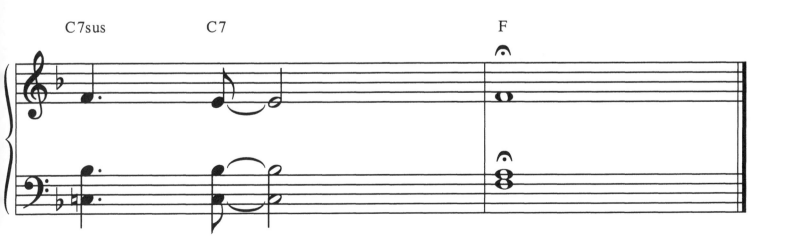

# STRAWBERRY FIELDS FOREVER

Words and Music by JOHN LENNON
and PAUL McCARTNEY

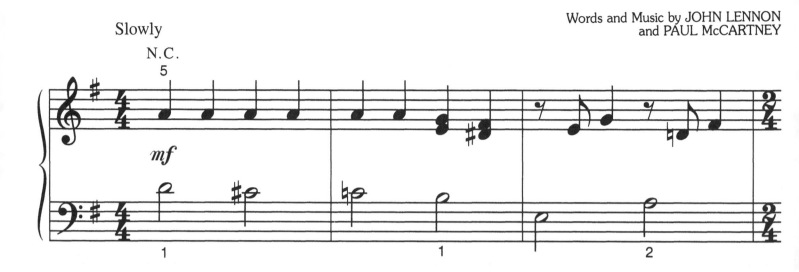

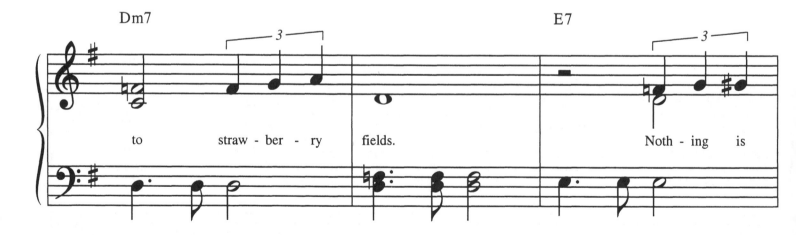

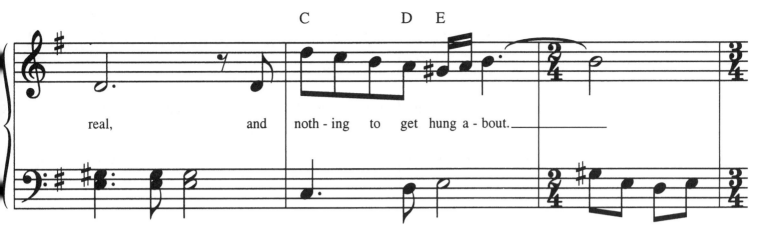

real, and noth-ing to get hung a-bout.

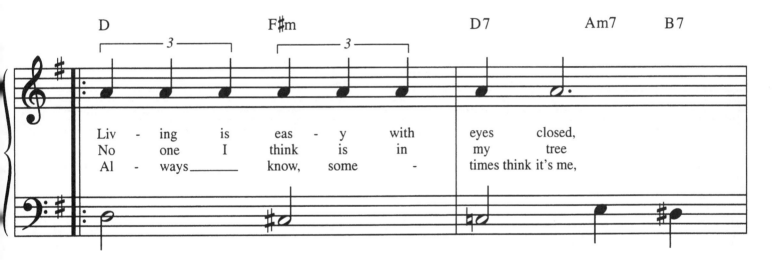

Straw-ber-ry fields for - ev - er.

Liv - ing is eas - y with eyes closed,
No one I think is in my tree
Al - ways know, some - times think it's me,

mis-un-der-stand-ing all you see.
I mean it must be high or low.
but you know I know when it's a dream.

It's get - ting hard to be some - one but it all___ works__ out,
That is, you know you can't tune in but it's all_____ right,
I think a "no" will be a "yes," but it's all_____ wrong,

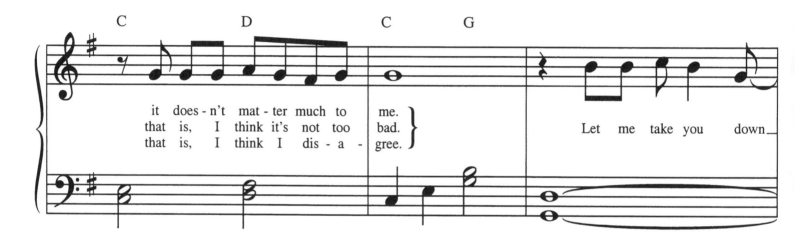

it does - n't mat - ter much to | me. }
that is, I think it's not too | bad. }
that is, I think I dis - a - | gree. }

Let me take you down__

___ 'cause I'm go - ing to straw - ber - ry fields.

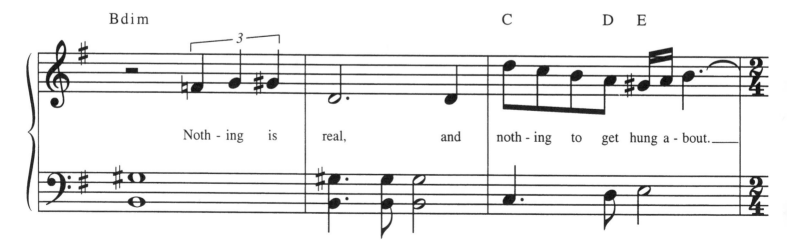

Noth - ing is real, and noth - ing to get hung a - bout.___

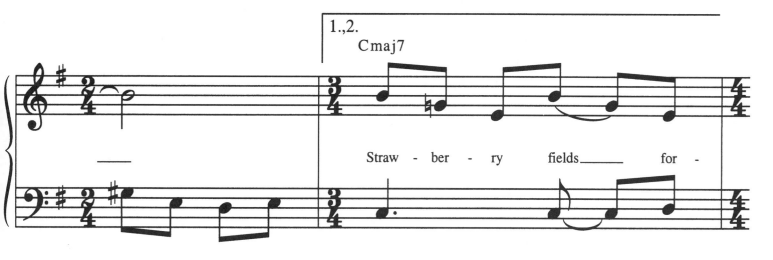

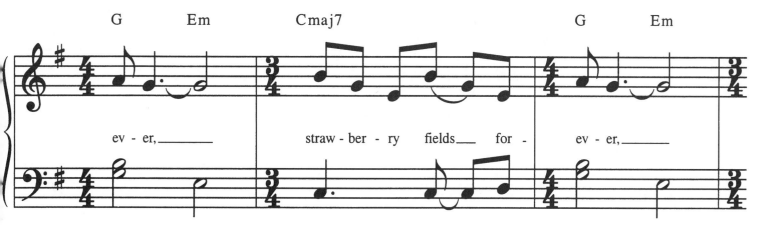

# TWIST AND SHOUT

Words and Music by BERT RUSSELL
and PHIL MEDLEY

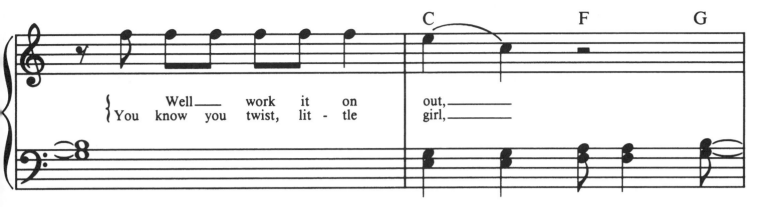

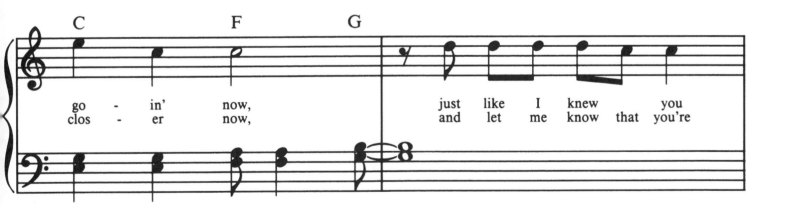

# YESTERDAY

Words and Music by JOHN LENNON
and PAUL McCARTNEY

I said some-thing wrong. Now I long for yes - ter -

day. _____ Yes-ter-day, love was such an eas - y

game to play. Now I need a place to hide a - way. Oh,

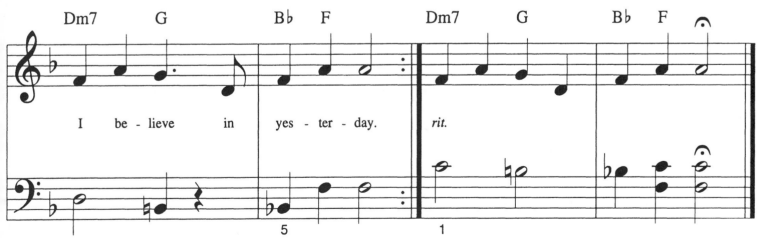

I be - lieve in yes - ter - day. *rit.*

# YOU'VE GOT TO HIDE YOUR LOVE AWAY

Words and Music by JOHN LENNON
and PAUL McCARTNEY

Moderately (each measure = 1 beat)

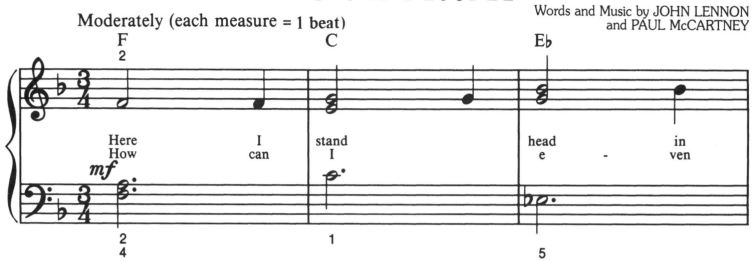

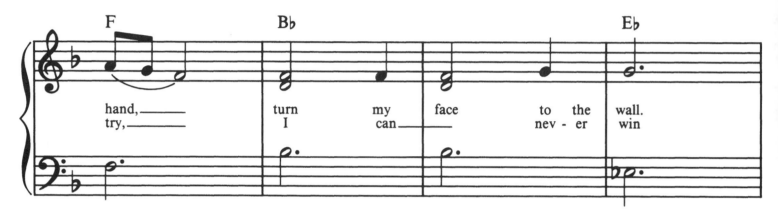

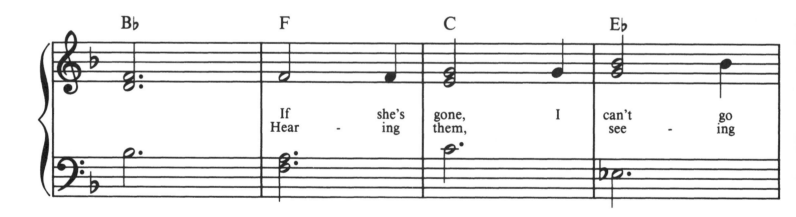

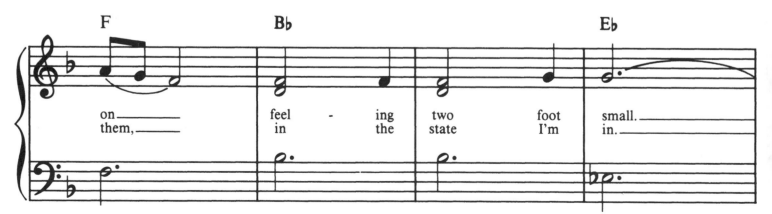

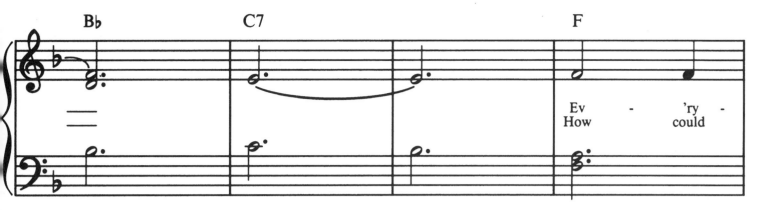

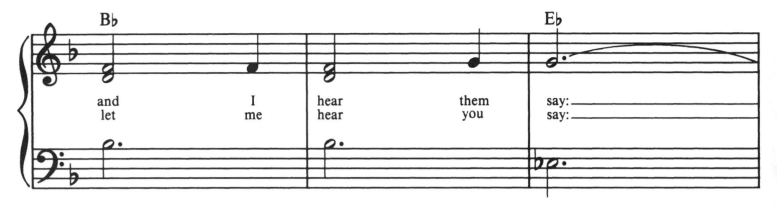

and let | I me | hear hear | them you | say: say:

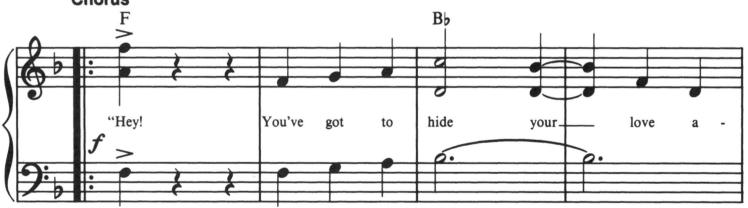

**Last time repeat chorus and fade**
**Chorus**

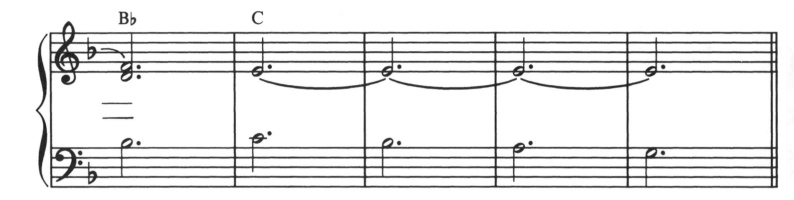

"Hey! | You've got to | hide your | love a -

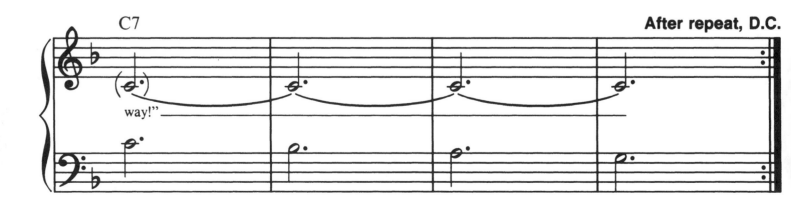

**After repeat, D.C.**

way!"